MYSTICAL CROONER:
The Lives of Leonard Cohen

by Aubrey Malone

Mystical Crooner: The Lives of Leonard Cohen

By Aubrey Malone

Wisdom Twin Books, 2025

Text Copyright of Aubrey Malone, 2025

Formatted by Eileen Lanigan

ISBN: 978-1-326-46802-6

All rights reserved. No part of this publication may be reproduced, stored in a retrieval system, or transmitted in any form or by any means, electronic, mechanical, photocopy, recording or otherwise, without prior written permission of the copyright owner. Nor can it be circulated in any form of binding or cover other than that in which it is published and without similar condition including this condition being imposed on a subsequent purchaser.

Mystical Crooner
The Lives of Leonard Cohen

CONTENTS

Introduction 5
Born Like This 7
Came So Far For Beauty 19
From Page to Stage 40
So Long, Marianne 49
Famous Blue Leonard 63
Spector of Doom 87
Crawling From the Wreckage 96
Back in the Game 107
Dublin Visit 130
Burn-Out 144
The Deal is Rotten 168
First We Take Fredericton 179
Closing Time 196
Aftermath 206
Notes 209
Bibliography 219

Introduction

My reverence for Leonard Cohen goes back to when he started out. Very few of the people I knew liked him as much as I did. Possession of his albums hardly went to the top of their bucket list. Neither were his novels or poems very popular with them.

I stayed with him through the lean years, buying copies of his books (usually remaindered ones) for a pittance. I endured people laughing at me when I brought his name up at fashionable cocktail parties. Sometimes I was glad when they laughed. It meant he was my possession alone.

There were times in the seventies and eighties when the words "Leonard" and "Cohen" couldn't be put in the same sentence without drawing howls of derision.

People trivialised him with cliches like "High Priest of Heartbreak." They ignored the fact that many of his songs were life-affirming. He just sang them an octave below the level of most singers.

He often thought his career was over before it had properly started but he kept on keeping on and eventually the tide turned. His enemies realised what they'd been missing. The rest of us just went on as we were.

It's often said that we shouldn't meet our heroes, that the gilt will rub off on our fingers, but when I interviewed Cohen in 1988 he was exactly what I expected him to be. A gentleman, and funny with it.

There was an air of affectionate formality about him. He deferred to me without appearing to, taking time to process everything I said, no matter how trivial it was. He crafted his answers to questions with the same precision as he did his poetry and songs. You knew that the better the question was, the more fascinating the answer would be, but that he'd even give thoughtful answers to poor questions. As with everything else he did in life, he gave interviews 100% of his attention. He was "the perfect offering."

I also found him to be an insightful analyst of the absurdities of life. In that sense he became the personification of the character in his songs, a character who guided me, and many other members of my generation, through whatever traumas we were going through.

Whether you were getting out of a relationship or getting into one, Cohen was your go-to person. He was both the fulcrum of your emotional furniture and the rock it perished on, both your salvation and your doom. You took a Kierkegaardian leap of faith into his world only half expecting to come out of it intact because you knew there were no half-measures with him. There was only you and your passion, flying blind into escape hatches or dead ends.

That's his legacy.

Born Like This

Cohen came from a family with various business interests and strict religious practices. Music-wise his early influences were a compendium of folk songs from a scrapbook, his father's music hall albums and the Yiddish songs he heard his mother singing around the house.

It's hard to believe he was born before Elvis Presley and that he lived to be almost twice his age. The location was an affluent suburb of Montreal, the date September 21, 1934. His ancestors were East European, his father Nathan a prosperous Jew who ran a clothing business.

Cohen always remained a snappy dresser, such habits ingrained in him from childhood. His sartorial elegance didn't always sit well with his bohemian aspirations but as he often said, "I don't look well in Levis." And he didn't. A pin-striped suit and a fedora suited his image far better, even if they carried overtones of smoked salmon socialism. He was born, he said, before the blue jean revolution.

Nathan's family had emigrated from Poland in the late nineteenth century. His father was able to quote the Torah almost verbatim. Leonard's family name, a variant of Kohen, translates as "High Priest."

Music was tied up with religion for him from youth. The songs he learned in the synagogue stayed with him just as those the young Elvis listened to in the First Assembly of God church in Tupelo when he was a three-year-old boy scrambling his way from his mother's arms up to the altar. Tupelo was wilder than Montreal by some margin but the same early influences cut deep into the two singers' souls.

Both of them were also very tied to their mothers. Leonard's – a Red Cross worker before she married – was called Masha. He had one sibling, a sister called Esther who was four years older than him. Their childhood was orderly. They got up at roughly the same time every morning, went to bed at roughly the same time every night, and dressed up for dinner.

The Cohens had an Irish maid called Mary and a black gardener, Kerry, who was also the family's chauffeur. The area they lived in was called Westmount. The only vaguely subversive thing the young Leonard did was hypnotise Mary one night and ask her to take off her clothes. In later years he was able to get women to do this without resorting to hypnosis – unless you call his singing hypnotic. It often was.

Bob Dylan, to whom he would often be compared throughout his career, once said that it was too cold to be a rebel where he grew up in the mining district of Hibbing, Minnesota. Everyone just did what their fathers and forefathers had done.

Cohen was also a conformist in his early years. "Sometimes I think I sleepwalked through my youth," he said. Shades of the prison house began to close about the growing boy.

Nathan died in 1944 aged just 52. He'd had bad health most of his life. He once told Leonard he never expected to live long.

After he was buried, Leonard wrote a poem to him. He went up to Nathan's bedroom and looked in one of his drawers. There he found a bow tie. He cut a wing from it and put the poem inside. Then he sewed it up. He buried the tie in his garden. It was his first poem and maybe, he thought afterwards, his most important one. He tried to find it some months later but couldn't, despite digging all over the garden. It was full of pansies. His father had always worn a pansy in his lapel so he felt this was appropriate.

Every poem he wrote afterwards, he claimed, was like a repeat of him digging around his garden as a nine-year-old boy looking for the tie he'd buried there with the elegy to his father sewn inside it. Seamus Heaney made a similar analogy between writing and excavation when he wrote in the poem "Digging" about excavating language with his "squat pen."

It was Esther's birthday the following day. Leonard was now the man of the house. He tried to cheer her up but he couldn't, neither her nor himself: "Every thought led them back to the funeral home."[1]

He didn't cry at his father's funeral but he did when his dog died a few years later. He thought this pointed to a lack of emotion in him. In more objective moments he thought it more likely that his lack of a reaction was caused by the fact that his father's poor health throughout his life meant his premature demise hadn't really come as a shock.

He believed his death helped him become more in touch with his feminine side. Cohen indulged this with his mother and sister. It tapped into his literary side as well. He always felt literature came from that part of one's personality.

In 1950 he became a counsellor at a Jewish community camp for children who couldn't afford much. Here he found a book called The People's Songbook. He browsed through it and liked what he saw. It contained songs by people like Woody Guthrie and Leadbelly as well as various Scottish melodies. He bought his first guitar in a second-hand pawnshop in Montreal for $12. When he was growing up, he said, anyone who played a guitar was seen as a communist.[2]

He graduated from Westmount High School in 1951. On his 17th birthday he enrolled at McGill University to study literature. He also did a semester at law. When he wasn't reading books he played rhythm guitar with a country and western musical group he formed with two of his friends called The Buckskin Boys. The only reason they called themselves by this name was because, by a strange coincidence, they all happened to own buckskin jackets.

They played anywhere they could find an audience: farmyard barns, high school auditoriums, church basements. Country music was a genre Cohen loved all his life and would like to have featured it more in his repertoire. He had a particular fascination for George Jones, and listened to him any time he could. Jones, he joked, was his "secret vice."

He was displaying eccentric traits even by this stage. After becoming president of the university's debating team he went on to ban all debates.[3]

His immersion in literature saw the first example of his individuality beginning to emerge. He left home and moved into a flat. This didn't go down well with his father, who'd lived at home until he was nearly thirty, leaving only to get married to Masha.

He read everything he could get his hands on, the world of books liberating him from what he now saw to be an insular environment in Montreal. Discovering the work of the Spanish poet Federico Garcia Lorca changed the life of the young Cohen completely.

Lorca appealed to him for all sorts of reasons. As well as loving his imagistic style of writing, he identified with his cultured upbringing, his love of music (Lorca was a pianist) and his left-wing political principles. These had cost him his life when he was mown down by the fascists during the Spanish Civil War.

His first experience of Lorca was in 1949. "This was the man who ruined my life," was the way he put it. He was mesmerised by him from the moment he took up one of his books. In later years he said, "I never left that world."[4] One of his favourite Lorca books was *Poet in New York*. He read it so much, the pages eventually started to fall out.

He felt Lorca helped him find his voice. He didn't copy him – nobody could – but reading him gave him the feeling that he too could be a writer.

The Spanish element found its way into Cohen's music by coincidence. One day when he was walking in a park in Westmount he spotted a young man playing songs on a guitar for some women. He became enchanted by the flamenco style he had and engaged him in conversation. His English was poor so this wasn't easy but he managed to get his phone number from him. He asked him if he would be willing to teach him to play. He said he would.

He pointed to his house, which was visible in the distance, to tell him where to go. He was poor during the first lesson. "You don't know how to play," the young man told him, "Let me show you." He placed Cohen's hands on the strings of his guitar and showed him how to pluck, to strum, to make chords. By the second lesson he was a little better. By the third he knew six chords.

"Those six chords," he said later, "formed the basis of all my music." They were especially applicable to his tremolo playing style.

His teacher didn't turn up for his fourth lesson. No reason was given. When he rang his boarding house he received the most shocking news anyone could: the young man had taken his life. Cohen hadn't even asked him his name.

Masha started to suffer from depression in the following years. It transmitted itself to Leonard as he struggled to find his voice and his vocation. His father's death and the suicide of his guitar teacher weighed heavily on him during these years.

Masha married a pharmacist called Harry Ostrow in 1950. Shortly after the wedding he was diagnosed with multiple sclerosis. She suspected he knew he had the condition before he married her. She'd spent too much of her life nursing Nathan to want to continue doing so with another man. This led to almost immediate tensions between the pair. The relationship was fraught but rumbled on until 1957, at which time they parted.

Cohen wasn't sure what he might do with his life after he graduated from the university. Masha wanted him to follow his father into the clothing trade but this didn't appeal to him.

He was spending a lot of time with his friend Mort Rosengarten now. Rosengarten had access to his father's car. At the dead of night the two of them patrolled the streets of Montreal looking for girls. They rarely found any. Who would be out at that hour, especially in the cold? But this was still an adventurous experience for Leonard. Searching for something, he thought, was often as exciting as finding it.

He wrote about this phase of his life with comic melodrama in his novel *The Favourite Game,* citing a time when he and his friend Krantz, who's loosely based on Rosengarten, specifically target two women. "He wonders how many miles through Montreal streets he and Krantz have driven and walked," he writes, "on the look-out for the two girls who had been chosen cosmically to be their companion-mistresses. Hot summer evenings casing the mobs in Lafontaine Park, looking searching into young female eyes, they knew that at any moment two beauties would dislodge themselves from the crowd and take them in their arms."

Cohen had problems getting off with women at this time. He felt he wasn't masculine enough. What did it say about him that his main literary influence was a gay man?

He was embarrassed by his short stature, imagining it would get in the way of any success he might otherwise have with women. In *The Favourite Game* Leonard had his hero Lawrence Breavman stuff his shoes with Kleenex one night before going out on a date.

The three years Cohen spent at university meant little to him. His main interest in being there, he said, was to explore the various delights of wine, women and song. "I hardly went to any of the classes," he confessed, "Nobody really cared whether you turned up or not."

At night he toured the musical bars with Rosengarten. During his third year, his literature class was given by the Polish-Canadian poet Louis Dudek. Dudek later became a friend of his. He was writing a lot at this time. Dudek admired his work so much he was said to have "knighted" Cohen one day using a rolled-up copy of one of his poems.[5]

In a less laudatory mood, Dudek was alleged to have dubbed his writings "a ragbag of classical mythology."[6] Lorca's voice was evident in many of them.

He graduated from McGill with a B.A. in 1955, thereafter doing a year in Law at Columbia University in New York. This did nothing for him. Back in Montreal he continued writing.

The biggest influence on him next to Lorca was the Canadian poet Irving Layton. He was 22 years older than him but he too became a friend in time.

Layton was the *enfant terrible* of Canadian literature. He had a gripping style but wrote too much. A lot of it was substandard. People felt it was worth wading through for the nuggets of genius.

Layton advised Cohen to break away from the stuffiness of Montreal. One of his favourite pieces of advice to him was, "are you sure you're doing the wrong thing?"[7] Cohen didn't worship at his feet as so many did, becoming a friend instead.

He saw Layton as a breath of fresh air on the poetic scene, regarding him in the same way he would view Charles Bukowski in later years – someone who took poetry out of its stuffy grooves and brought it into the real world. The fact that both men looked more like fighters than writers fortified this appraisal of them for him.

Layton was Canada's most famous poet at this time. As an acquaintance remarked, "There was Irving and then there was the rest of us."[8] Cohen loved his work and the feeling was mutual. "Leonard was already a genius when we met," Layton extolled.[9]

He published his first book of poetry in 1956, *Let us Compare Mythologies*. "There are some really good poems in that little book," he joked years later, "It's been downhill ever since." The publishers were McClelland & Stewart. Jack McClelland, who went on to become a friend, accepted it almost on sight. Such was Cohen's reputation even this early.

Cohen never signed a contract with McClelland. He didn't say why and McClelland never pushed it. It meant he controlled all the rights to his poems. It's unlikely, however, that this was the reason for his behaviour. Its more likely he simply wasn't bothered.

It was an exciting time for literature. Allen Ginsberg had published *Howl and Other Poems* in 1956. *On the Road* came out the following year. Its original title was *The Beat Generation.* Cohen admired the Beats but he knew he could never be a part of them: "I was writing very rhymed, polished verses and they were in open revolt against that kind of form, which they associated with the oppressive literary establishment."[10]

Sometimes when he read his poems to audiences they sounded like prayers even when the content wasn't overly spiritual. This probably resulted from his experience of reading from the Bible in the synagogue.

Not all of these audiences were receptive to what he wrote. Some hailed him as the "golden boy" of Canadian poetry, the new Layton if you like, while others thought he was pretentious and above himself.

He found an element of begrudgery in Montreal that upset him. One day he was putting an envelope into a letterbox when a man came up to him. He said, "I bet there's not a decent poem in that envelope."[11] It was a gratuitous insult based on nothing but jealousy. He hadn't even been mailing a poem at the time, merely a letter.

"In Canada," he complained, "people can't accept the fact that anything good can come out of a neighbour's house." He added with his familiar black humour, "Everyone is unhappy in Canada and if they're not unhappy they're dull. It's a wonderful place to write."[12]

He didn't know if he was a genuine poet or not. Was he entitled to say one way or the other? He didn't believe a person could call themselves a poet. It was a verdict others gave.[13] You weren't a poet just because the lines didn't reach the end of the page.[14]

He spent most of 1956 in New York. He felt like a fish out of water there, at least until he met a young woman called Georgianna Sherman. She was very attractive and he fell head over heels in love with her. He spent most of the next eighteen months with her. In the summer of 1957 he took her to Quebec to meet Layton and his wife Aviva. They were equally charmed by her.

Sherman was his first time dating a gentile. He gave himself to her in a way that was indicative of his early excitability, throwing himself at her unconditionally. "Let's run away," he gushed in a letter he wrote to her, "Let's go native in Ottawa. Let's meet in Central Station and kiss shamelessly in front of all the trains."[15]

"Anna" as he called her, became the template for the character of Shell in *The Favourite Game.* When she expressed a wish to marry him, however, he withdrew from her.

The institution always scared him. Sherman wrote years later in a poem that love – not marriage, mind – was "a burden he couldn't take on."

He went back to his home in Montreal after the relationship broke up. His grandfather, Rabbi Klonitzki-Kline, was living there now with his mother, but suffering from Alzheimer's Disease. Cohen featured him in a novel he started before *The Favourite Game, A Ballet of Lepers.* He'd been a writer in his own youth and saw Leonard as a kindred soul. Sometimes he'd pass him in the house. If he was having a lucid interval he'd go, "Ah, the writer" as if he was carrying on the family tradition.

Cohen was also writing a third novel now, one called *Beauty at Close Quarters.* This has never surfaced. Because of the simultaneous nature of the three books, Cohen came to refer to *The Favourite Game* as "a third novel masquerading as a first one."

He became consumed by the writing of it, setting a number of hours aside for it each day. There was a clock on his desk which had the glass missing. Sometimes he moved the time forward with his hand when he needed to get away from it. The difficulty of writing it was reflected in a turgid tone it carried throughout. It was this that led to it being rejected by any publishers he sent it to. These rejections hurt him deeply.

The feeling that he wouldn't be able to "make it" as a writer resulted in him working in a foundry in 1957. This was never going to be anything more than a stopgap and he soon tired of it. One day he sat down at a card table on a sun porch and started writing a poem. The experience gave him "mastery and power."[16]

The "card table" poem, like the bow tie one of his youth, became a watershed for him. It strengthened the notion in him that he could become a writer. He tried to put the rejection of *A Ballet of Lepers* out of his mind and work on something else. That something else became *The Favourite Game*.

The book gives us the first inkling of how music was going to become a central part of his life if and when literature failed to fulfil him fully: "His guitar was always handy. The cedar wood was cool against his stomach. The inside of the guitar smelled like the cigar boxes his father used to have. The tone was excellent in the middle of the night. In those late hours the purity of the music surprised and almost convinced him that he was creating a sacramental relationship with the girl, the city, and himself."

In 1959 he received a grant of $2000 from the Canadian Council for the Arts. This enabled him to go to London. On the day he arrived he bought an Olivetti typewriter and a Burberry coat, the one that would become the "famous blue raincoat" of his song.

He told the landlady of the boarding house at which he was staying, Stella Pullman, about his novel. She became interested in it. He said it was a very intensive work and that he could only write three pages a day. She said she understood this but that he owed it

17

to himself to meet that target. If he didn't, she teased, she wouldn't allow him to stay with her.

He gravitated between London and Montreal that year, wondering how his life in writing was going to pan out. He wasn't sure if he could make a living from it. With Layton he went through a spell of writing plays for TV but they went nowhere.

Afterwards they got a better idea. They started writing bogus letters to one another that they sold to a university for $25 each. Aviva crumpled the pages to make them look old. The con job made more for them than their plays ever would have. Somebody once said the only way to make money from writing was to write ransom notes. This came a close second for the two fraudsters.

Came So Far For Beauty

The longer Cohen spent in London, the more the weather started to get him down. One day in an effort to escape from a shower – one of the near-permanent ones in the city – he sheltered in the doorway of a bank. Seeing a suntanned cashier inside and wondering how he came by the tan, he asked him where he'd been.

"I've just come back from Greece," he told him, "The weather was glorious there." Cohen booked a flight for Athens the very next day. From there he went to the island of Hydra, which he'd heard was a kind of haven for artists and writers. The decision was unusually impetuous for him. It would have enormous repercussions.

He never saw Canada as suiting his personality, saying "I belong beside the Mediterranean. My ancestors made a terrible mistake."

He fell in love with Hydra immediately. The white houses, the winding streets; such things provided him with the ideal writing – and living – environment. There were no televisions there, and precious few cars. That added to its allure for him.

Henry Miller had once lived there calling it a "promised land" that caused him to lose "all sense of earthly direction." [2]

Miller rhapsodised about the "flawless anarchy" and the "wild and naked perfection" of Hydra when he was there in 1939. There were only two colours on the island, he maintained, blue and white, "and the white is whitewashed every day."

Cats slept on the rocks, stretching their paws as they woke. Cohen enjoyed their laziness. He was entranced by the horseshoe-shaped harbour, the slow pace of living, the sun that bathed everyone in its glow. Everywhere he looked there were stone streets, rocky hillsides. Many of the houses were uninhabited. There were no cars. The streets were too narrow for them. Motorcycles were also banned. Only rubbish trucks were allowed. People lounged around outside the bars, laughing and arguing as if there was no tomorrow. In their world, maybe there wasn't. He liked watching the sun going down over the empty harbour as the waves lapped against the shore.

Donkeys lurched along the cobbled streets and up the rocky slopes with their burdens, carrying people and goods to selected destinations.

He met an Australian couple, George Johnston and his wife Charmian Clift. They found a house he could rent. Both of them were writers. He became friends with them, feeling a fellowship with their situation. They lived modestly and told him he could too. He hung his coat on the door and put his typewriter on the table, anxious to begin his new life.

Apart from an hour of electricity in the morning and an hour at night, he was dependent on candles for light. They were a much better aid to inspiration for a poet than anything he'd had in Montreal. The only transport was the donkeys. He had to bribe the garbage man to take out his trash.[3] There was no running water.

"Hydra" literally meant water, which made its scarcity ironic. An earthquake was said to have deprived the island of it. The term was also a reference to the doorman of Hades in Greek mythology.

He lived largely on credit. People were happy to let him. There was that laidback attitude even in the stores. "Leonardo" could always be trusted to pay when he had the money. A trust fund of an annual $750 from his father's will helped him survive financially. There were also some royalties from his books. His grandmother died at the end of that summer, leaving him $1500 in her will.

On September 27th, six days after his 26th birthday, Cohen bought a house with the inheritance money. The number was 764. This was a curiosity among its many other curiosities as there were only a few other houses on the street.

Sequestered away in his hideaway home he got down to pounding the keys of his Olivetti. The words poured out of him as he embarked on a series of poems.

He wrote to his mother too, letting her know how he was doing, like any dutiful son. He said he was practicing the old dictum of, as he put it, "a sound mind in a sound body." He got up every morning at 7:30 and then worked for three hours. In the afternoons he swam and lay in the sun. The view from his house was beautiful. He watched "the harbour, and then the Mediterranean."[4]

He would soon watch something else even more beautiful – the woman who would become the centre of his life for the next five years, a Norwegian called Marianne Ihlen. He met her outside the shop where he bought most of his provisions. It was run by two people, the Katsikas brothers. The shop doubled as a post office.

The first time he talked to her was a day when she was shopping for food. He was outside the shop with some of his friends. She had a basket in her hands. Her first sight of him was in silhouette, the sun blocking her vision.

"Would you like to join us?" he asked, "We're sitting outside." She was captivated by his voice, not having heard a Canadian accent before.

Her grandmother, who'd raised her in Oslo, always told her she would meet a man "who spoke with a tongue of gold." Now she was hearing it. She remembered him wearing what she called a

21

"sixpence" cap and having the sleeves of his shirt rolled up. "When my eyes met his," she said, "I felt it throughout my body."[5]

She was so happy to meet him, she danced all the way home. She'd felt an almost electrical charge radiating through her when she talked to him. He was enraptured with her too.

"I didn't think I was much to look at," she said, "I didn't believe him when he said I was the most beautiful woman he ever saw."[6] Cohen didn't think he was handsome either. Both of them were more praising of the other than they were of themselves – a good formula for a relationship.

He'd seen her with her husband and baby many times before he spoke to her. He thought they looked like the perfect family. Both father and son were called Axel. The father's surname was Jensen. Like Cohen he was a writer. They'd been on the island two years.

Marianne was working in an attorney's office in Oslo when she met Jensen. He appeared exciting to her in contrast to the drudgery of her job. When he asked her to go to Greece with him she was overjoyed. Her parents disapproved as they had no plans to marry at that point but she wasn't to be deterred.

He was mistaken about them being a perfect family. At this time Marianne wasn't long back from Oslo after giving birth to Axel. While she was away, Jensen had started sleeping with an American artist called Patricia Amlin. It wasn't his first infidelity. He'd just told Marianne he was going to leave her for Amlin. He wanted a divorce.

Cohen met her a few times after the rendezvous outside the shop. They became good friends. At this stage he didn't know it was going to become a romantic relationship. Soon afterwards it did. When that happened, she moved into his house with him. Amlin later had a terrible car accident in Athens. Jensen was so shocked by the extent of her injuries he couldn't even visit her in hospital. It was left to Marianne to do this.

A lesser woman than she would have said to Amlin after her accident, "It's no more than you deserve." Instead, she deputised for her ex-husband in going to visit her. She'd broken many bones. There was also gangrene in her thumb. It had to be amputated.

Soon afterwards Marianne had to go to Oslo for her divorce proceedings. Cohen went with her. Both of them were glad that there was going to be closure on her broken marriage, that they'd be able to concentrate on their own relationship.

After they came back from Oslo they felt closer than ever. They went swimming by day and lit fires at night, watching the shadows dance on the walls as the flames rose. There was very little electricity on the island. People had to use candles or oil lamps for light.

Cohen felt rejuvenated when he swam. Tamar Hodes had him saying in a novel she wrote about him living in Hydra, "When you come out of the sea here you're covered in plankton, your body shining as if you've become someone else."[7]

Life was simple for them. They collected shells on the sand. They watched the tide go in and out. They bought groceries from the Katsikas brothers like "ordinary folks." There was no class structure on Hydra, Being a writer was the same as being a fisherman.

Marianne wondered how Cohen would be with Axel as he grew. She needn't have been. At times he was even a better parent to him than she was. When he cried, he invited him into his study to "help" him with his work.

His life with Marianne was near-idyllic. He happily slotted into the position Jensen had been in at the beginning of his relationship with Marianne, becoming a surrogate father to the boy.

He had some problems communicating with him at first as he only spoke Norwegian but the warmth between them over-rode this obstacle. Marianne also experienced that warmth. It was such a contrast to Jensen. She was able to express herself with Cohen without any inhibitions.

She hadn't always been like this. The product of a traditional childhood in a conservative country, she was able to be a free spirit in Hydra in a way that wouldn't have been tolerated in Oslo. Here she was still happy to subjugate herself to her man, be that Jensen or Cohen. She liked her identity as home-maker, mother, lover.

They did childish things together. One day after having a bath, Cohen put his typewriter under the water to see if he could type on it that way. The experiment only had limited success. A bigger surprise was the fact that it didn't wreck his machine.

Another day he wrote on a wall: "I change. I am the same. I change. I am the same." Cohen said once, "What I admire in the morning I despise by sundown." "Change," he claimed, was "the only aphrodisiac."

He was able to live on $1000 a year. This meant the royalties that arrived in the mail were enough to put bread on the table. Marianne did some modelling, which also helped.

Marianne had a complex about the fact that she wasn't artistic. Most of the people she knew were writers, artists, sculptors. Now she had a singer to boot. "Life was my art," she said, "It was all I had to work with." For Cohen, however, it was more than enough.

Cohen published a poetry collection, *The Spice Box of Earth*, in 1961, again with Jack McClelland. He also went to Cuba that year. Fidel Castro had come into power. Violence was everywhere. He wondered if he might be struck in an air raid. "What great publicity!" he said to McClelland.[8]

Architecturally the country was in ruins. He walked through the bombed-out streets with a kind of curious fascination. Castro had just overthrown former dictator Fulgensio Batista in a major coup. Cohen was excited by it all but as an emigrant from a capitalist country he was clearly in the wrong place at the wrong time. Even Ernest Hemingway had departed Cuba at this point, despite having spent some of the happiest years of his life there.

Cohen was there for a number of reasons. Lorca had visited it. Esther had honeymooned there two years before. She'd been in ecstasies about its exciting night life. Cohen wanted to see if Castro might have changed that. "I am wild for all kinds of violence," he pronounced, "I thought maybe this was my Spanish Civil War."[9] It was difficult to take his pronouncement seriously. He grew a beard like Che Guevara – which got him into trouble with the authorities – but he was never going to be a militant.

Did he think he was? He made some noises that way but more often he was jocose, especially when he described himself as the "last tourist" in the country in a poem.

The Bay of Pigs Incident broke out while he was there. It made his situation more complicated. All the airports were closed so he stayed. He was seen as a bourgeois anarchist by some, the kind of person who might write a song about a cause but not get his hands dirty. Though he made the Hemingwayesque pronouncement "I wanted to kill or be killed," he didn't see any action. He'd like to have met Hemingway. He was disappointed that he'd gone from a place that had been so dear to him for so long.

His presence in the country suggested to one writer that he was trying to model himself on George Orwell in Catalonia during the Spanish Civil War.[10] "All of South America is on the threshold of revolution," he wrote to Marianne. The incendiary atmosphere made literature seem trivial by comparison. "Sometimes I look at my poems," he wrote, "and feel quite obsolete."[11]

Cohen left Cuba after an official from the Canadian embassy informed him that his mother was worried about him. That wasn't a good look for the would-be revolutionary. His street cred was salvaged somewhat when he was detained by armed soldiers at Havana airport after they discovered a photograph in his luggage of him posing with some revolutionary soldiers.

He evaded further detention by slipping out of the airport when the soldiers' attention was diverted by a scuffle on the runway. This prevented a possible imprisonment. They thought he was American rather than Canadian. That could have compromised his status as a "tourist."

Other departures from Hydra were less dramatic. He left the island every so often when, as he put it, he needed to renew his "neurotic affiliations."[12]

Now and then he went back to Canada to earn a buck. "I worked in an office," he told an interviewer, "I ran an elevator. I did a great deal of journalism. I sold some short stories."[13] They paid for his "pure" life back with his beloved Marianne back on his dream island.

Cohen always romanticised Marianne, not only in song but whenever he spoke about her. It wasn't only her beauty that captivated him but her constant good humour and her modesty – a quality she shared with him. In an interview once he spoke of a moment when he was as happy with her as he'd ever been with anyone. It was when he was about to board a ferry with her to go back to Hydra after being away from the island for a time. They hailed a taxi. He sat in and lit a cigarette.

He thought: "I'm with this beautiful woman and I have a little money in my pocket. He never experienced such a feeling of unadulterated happiness again no matter how hard he tried. It was the simplicity of it that got to him. "All the world is in front of you," he told the interviewer, "Your body is suntanned, and you're going to get on a boat."[14]

Cohen wrote many of his most evocative songs when he was with Marianne. "So Long, Marianne" was the most obvious one.

He also wrote "Hey, That's No Way To Say Goodbye" there, and "Bird on the Wire." The original title of "So Long Marianne" was "Come On, Marianne." He hadn't written it as a farewell song. That came later. He changed Marianne's name from its original "Marianna" so that it would scan better. He says in the course of it, "I see you've gone and changed your name again" but it was actually Cohen who did this.

Marianne described how "Bird on the Wire" came about. He had flu at the time. It was early in the morning. When he got up he saw that during the night electric wires had been installed on the street in front of the window, obstructing their view of the harbour. He was upset by this but then he saw some birds landing on them – like, as Marianne put it, "notes on a music sheet." Their arrival lit a spark to his muse. He began singing the words, "Like a bird, on the wire." Marianne was mesmerized. Cohen had been undergoing writer's block at the time. The song got him out of it.

It was a wonderful song but it came at a price. After the wires went up, it was like the death knell to his pure lifestyle. He kept looking out the window at them thinking how civilization had caught up with him: "I wasn't going to be able to live this 11th century life that I thought I'd found for myself anymore."[15] Up until then he'd seen himself as someone "in the court of Ferdinand, singing my songs to girls over a lute."[16]

The arrival of electricity changed Cohen's life on Hydra in a number of ways. It meant he could receive phone calls from publishers now. On the negative side, it meant Masha was in touch with him a lot more.

He started "Bird on the Wire" on Hydra but didn't finish it until three years later. Many songs he wrote were never finished, merely abandoned. If he couldn't get a rhyme or a reflection right he preferred to stuff the intended song or poem in a drawer rather than release it.

"Bird on the Wire" became one of his most-loved songs. Kris Kristofferson thought so much of it he said he wanted its opening lines to be inscribed on his grave. He leavened his praise by remarking that he thought Cohen had "stolen" its melody from Lefty Frizell's "Mom and Dad's Waltz." The two songs are definitely alike but it's difficult to imagine Cohen being aware of this, or imagine him lowering himself to such plagiarism.

Hydra gave him an ideal working environment but the island hardly features at all in his work. It was his catalyst rather than his raw material.

When he was writing there he often did so to the backing of music. Ray Charles was a particular favourite. He said he would have "killed" to have a voice like his. He also played a U.S. service station and, as mentioned, George Jones – his "secret vice."

How could he like the redneck's favourite? Did it not clash with everything he'd represented since leaving the Buckskin Boys? Or was that country-lovin', ass-kickin' music still lodged somewhere in his gut? Jones himself would have been discombobulated if he heard Cohen had listed his song "I Stopped Lovin' Her Today" as one of his favourites, or other cheesy numbers like "Why Do Fools Fall in Love."

After he finished writing for the day he used to go down to the pier and sit watching the boats. Young girls often collected themselves around him. Marianne would be filled with envy but she couldn't do anything about it. He didn't fend them off, flattered by their attentions. She wondered if the day would come when he'd go off with one of them, for a day or forever. She had to live with that fear.

Cohen went missing for hours, even days, and Marianne put up with it. She didn't know if he was with other women or not and she didn't dare ask. There was a risk she'd drive him away from her. She sometimes wished she could put a cage around him and swallow the key. She was more relaxed when he was working even if he didn't talk to her much during these times.

He lived a quiet life with her. They enjoyed drinking together but he rarely drank to excess. He described himself as a sloppy drunk: "I just get kind of stupid and throw up."[17] But he found it fun to be in the presence of other people who were drinking heavily. If he didn't join them he was able to keep his mind clear for the next day's work.

He set the alarm for dawn every day so he could work when it was at its most alert. After lunch he had a siesta or swam.

Marianne put a gardenia on his desk every morning to entice him to work. Some mornings he didn't want to but she told him he should. She'd been the same with Jensen. She was now a literary muse for the second time.

Later on in the morning she brought him tea. She knew better than to say anything when she left it on his desk. His concentration was always so intense.

He was intense when he was singing as well, becoming so involved in the activity it was as if he was in a trance.

When she listened to him singing she became as immersed in his world as he was, hypnotised by his words. But then the song ended and they were back to reality. He became her lover again instead of Leonard Cohen the singer. She watched him switching from his typewriter to his guitar with a mixture of awe and amusement. Was he a singer or a writer? Could you be both?

He plinked his guitar for her and her son over the long winter evenings, his susurrating melodies lulling Axel to sleep so they could have time to themselves.

Sometimes they travelled to Piraeus, coming back with oriental rugs and fine linen. One day they bought an antique mirror to hang in the hall.

He gave her gifts that he chose especially for her – a tortoiseshell mirror, a pair of scissors shaped like a bird with the blades at its beak, a collection of poems by Lorca.[18]

She'd love to have had a child by him. It would have given some kind of permanence to their relationship. Was it a possibility? She didn't know.

A writer who knew Cohen and Marianne in Hydra claimed she became pregnant many times by him. There was little birth control on the island. The "pill" was rarely given to unmarried couples at this time, even in "liberal" Hydra. The writer said Cohen didn't want Marianne to have his child, saying, "It's not the right time." Marianne thought his problem was that she wasn't Jewish and he wanted a Jewess to mother his children. (There was a question mark over the Jewishness of the woman who eventually would).[19]

Cohen wanted his life to remain exactly like it was, with Marianne as his lover without any strings. He wrote to his mother in 1962, "The secret of my triumph is that I expect nothing, expect to change nothing and expect to leave nothing behind."[20]

Marianne didn't put any pressure on him to marry her any more than she did to have his child. Marriage for many men was a logical extension of a love affair but for Cohen it signified entrapment: wedlock. Marianne was his great friend and lover as well as being his *femme inspiratrice* but she didn't "push" marriage, perhaps because the one to Jensen hadn't worked out. That suited Cohen.

Cohen's mother visited them in the summer of 1962. She was nervous about the visit, telling Cohen she was afraid the weather might be bad. Cohen told her it hadn't rained in 6000 years during the summer in Hydra so she'd probably be all right that way. When she suggested bringing a fur coat with her he told her (continuing his predilection for exaggeration) that if she did she'd probably be eaten by "several thousand cats" who'd never seen a fur coat before and would probably mistake her for some kind of animal.[21]

When she enquired about the house he told her it was big enough for her to share with his "several wives, mistresses and children"[22] His jocularity was snuffed out when he realised he'd have to move Marianne out of it for the duration of her stay. It was against Masha's

31

morals to see her son living with a woman, especially a divorced one who was a *goyim*.

The visit was a disaster for these and other reasons. Cohen was frustrated to be apart from Marianne and even more frustrated that Masha was cutting in on his writing regime. He was trying to revise *The Favourite Game* at the time and couldn't concentrate with her there.

He didn't relish visitors in general and discouraged them with a "Do Not Disturb" sign outside his door. He liked socialising at night but some of the people who visited were time-consuming. They didn't understand how seriously he took his writing. There were also the "groupies.'

He liked talking to young girls as long as they didn't ask him too many questions about his work. There was a danger of killing ideas if you over-thought them, or shared too many of them with others. "A writer should write his books," as Hemingway said, "and not talk about them."

McClelland & Steward rejected the first version of *The Favourite Game*. The company was more interested in him as a poet than a novelist. It was of course in this guise that he'd first presented himself to them, and to Canada. Not every poet could make a successful transition to another genre. Could Cohen? The novel was so abstruse they weren't sure. Neither, to be fair, was he. That fact meant he took the rejection in good part. "It will make me write better," he told Marianne, "This is new territory for me."

Writing a novel obviously took more concentration – and time – than writing a poem or a song: "You need one room, one table, one chair, one woman."[23]

He recounts many of the seminal episodes of his young life in the book – the cutting of his father's bow tie to sew the poem inside, the hypnosis of the family maid, etc. – leading us to see it as an autobiography. This was something he vehemently denied. The emotions were autobiographical, he emphasised, not the incidents. This flies in the face of the facts.

He invited more comparisons to his life by calling his main character Lawrence. It was too close to Leonard for comfort. The fact that his mother over-feeds him in one chapter, and kisses the family cardiologist in another one, angered Masha. "Is she me?" she wanted to know.

Cohen never answered questions like these but he was aware they posed problems with the book. When it was eventually published in 1963 he described it as "a miserable but important mess."[24] Canada was desperate to have a Keats figure, he alleged, which was why he wrote it.

He was also at work on another poetry book at this time, *Flowers for Hitler*. Marianne surprised him one day by coming home from Katsikas' post office with a copy of it. He'd dedicated it to her. It contains some fond tributes to her. A few of the poems were also general ones about his life in Hydra. He rarely wrote about his life there. The publisher, again, was McClelland & Stewart.

The original title he gave the book was *Opium and Hitler*. He told McClelland it would appeal to "the disclosed adolescents who compose my public."[25] McClelland thought this too inflammatory. In the end Cohen agreed to change it but he wasn't happy with the revised title. In many ways it was too cute. Even if he weren't Jewish, he knew readers would twig the fact that these are obviously going to be Baudelaire's "fleurs de mal."

33

Flowers for Hitler was a more ambitious book than *The Spice Box of Earth*. In it he tackled themes like Nazism and the Cold War. As such, it left him open to more criticism from reviewers. He was departing the "safe" academic realm for *realpolitik*. It was very important to him, as is evident from him saying to McClelland, "There has never been a book like this, either poetry or prose, written in Canada." He was fed up writing books "that would make everyone happy."

The book, he said, moved him from the world of the "golden boy poet" to the "dung pile of the frontline writer."[26] Exposure to the wider world always had a price for him. This was his first experience of paying it.

He was working on a second novel now. *Beautiful Losers* was an experimental work that explored his sexual obsession with a 17th century Mohawk woman called Catherine Tekakwitha.

Tekakwitha was Canada's first native saint. Cohen was fascinated by her. He used to lay flowers at a statue of her that was in St. Patrick's Cathedral in New York. She was only 24 when she died.

If *Flowers for Hitler* unpicked the Holocaust. *Beautiful Losers* was more like Eliot's *The Waste Land* crossed with Dante's *Inferno* - with some of Jean-Paul Sartre's *Nausea* thrown in for good measure.

He described it as "a love story, a psalm, a Black Mass, a monument, a satire, a prayer, a shriek, a road map through the wilderness, a joke, a tasteless affront, a bore."[27] It was limned with a conjunction of sacred and profane material. There was an element of the sophomore about the sexual passages in the book. It was as if he was trying to wave a finger of rebellion at his austere ancestry.

It showed the influence of James Joyce in its stream-of-consciousness style. There's also some D.H. Lawrence in there, courtesy of his manic dissertations with himself.

His writing seemed contradictory to the demeanour he generally displayed to his friends. He dressed soberly. His manners were unfailingly polite. He rose early. His routines were orderly but his books were wild. He gave off an aura of cool dignity while writing with the abandon of a Kerouac or a Ginsberg.

He wrote *Beautiful Losers* under the influence of hash, sometimes spending up to twenty hours a day on it. Ray Charles, as ever, gave him musical accompaniment. He listened to Charles' album *The Genius Sings the Blues* until the record warped in the sun.[28] For many of the later passages of the book, the speed seems to be doing the writing instead of Cohen.

He broke out in a fever when he finished it. Marianne put him to bed, soothing his hot forehead with a wet cloth and closing the shutters on the windows to keep the daylight out. Cohen had been on a ten-day fast. The shock to his system of the substance abuse, followed by the monastic style deprivation, resulted in a severe shock to his system. At one stage his temperature soared to 104 degrees.

He spent a week in hospital hallucinating. "One afternoon," he recalled, "the sky was black with storks. They alighted on all the churches and left in the morning. And I was better."[29]

Beautiful Losers was overwritten and overwrought, seeking to impress rather than express. It had moments of great poetry but for too much of the time it seemed to wallow in its indigestibility. "The burlesque element is overdone," one reviewer of it sniped, "and the pop art use of comic strips and junky advertisements were already old hat by the time of publication."[30]

It received mainly disastrous reviews. "The most revolting book ever written in Canada" screamed the *Toronto Daily Star*. "Verbal masturbation" was the appraisal of *The Globe and Mail*.

Gladys Taylor wrote in the *Toronto Telegram*, "I have just read Leonard Cohen's new novel and have to wash my mind." Such negative reviews killed any chance he had of making money from it. *The Boston Globe* was kinder, writing, "James Joyce is not dead. He is living in Montreal under the name Leonard Cohen."

That last burst was actually his farewell to the genre. He'd never attempt another novel. They were too time-consuming, too draining on his mental energies. The financial rewards were also practically non-existent. He enjoyed writing *The Favourite Game* but *Beautiful Losers* was more like an ordeal. Its lukewarm reception depressed him further,

Cohen had envisaged a different career for himself after putting everything of himself into these two novels. One might say the same for Philip Larkin, who thought he was going to be a novelist before poetry gripped him. Both men wrote two novels in relatively quick succession and then no more. Larkin devoted himself exclusively to poetry after his novels received disappointing reviews.

Cohen, like Larkin, had been mixing things up between his novels and poetry up to now. He didn't think his poems would stand the test of time when they were put up against major figures like Yeats and Tennyson. "I'll be lucky if I'm a footnote," he told his friend Barrie Wexler, "It's like going up against Muhammad Ali if you're a pretty good neighbourhood boxer."[31]   On the other hand, they took less out of him. From that point of view they were "the way to go."

Cohen had built up something of a reputation for himself by now, so much so that the National film Board of Canada commissioned a documentary about him. *Ladies and Gentlemen…..Mr Leonard Cohen* was a fly-on-the-wall film that showed him walking down streets, sitting in hotel rooms, reading his poetry at academic gatherings, jotting down reflections about life in little notebooks. It even showed him asleep, and in his bath.

He entered into the spirit of it wholeheartedly, saying he'd always had a yearning to be "discovered," he claimed, "like Hedy Lamarr in that drug store on Sunset Boulevard."[32] He probably meant Lana Turner at the soda fountain. He was, in any case, being frivolous. One can't imagine a writer less hungry for that kind of exposure.

He published another book of poetry, *Parasites of Heaven,* in 1966 but it didn't sell any better than his previous ones. A few thousand copies weren't enough to build a career on.

Things started to get complicated with Marianne now. Apart from his writing taking him away from her, there were other women. She tried to turn a blind eye to them.

She was also worried about the drugs he was taking to help him with his writing. LSD was rampant on the island. According to some people, it was even being given to the donkeys.

Hydra was a hotbed of permissiveness. As well as the drugs, everyone was sleeping with everyone. Cohen's friend Halle Goldman said, "very few marriages survived that place."

Some days he locked himself in his room as he wrote. She felt shut out. No longer did she place gardenias on his table to inspire him. She started to worry that she was losing her attractiveness to him. "I have no boobs," she complained.

He was trying to get his musical career off the ground. That obviously couldn't happen if he stayed in Hydra. He'd been travelling to Canada off and on for years. It was time to commit himself exclusively to where producers lived.

She thought he'd desert her when he went back to Montreal but he didn't. Instead he wrote her a telegram: "Have house. All I need now is my woman and her son. Love Leonard." She wasn't sure if he was summoning her from need or a sense of duty. "He needed to say it but he didn't mean it," she said afterwards. [33]

He met her at the airport a few days later. As she came down the runway she was carrying two valises. She couldn't wave to him with her hands so she did so with her foot instead. He was highly amused.

Axel didn't settle in Montreal. When he visited Aviva Layton, he wrote his name on every wall in her apartment. It was like a cry for help. Marianne became very distressed. She got a job in a boutique as Cohen tried to forge a career. Their relationship went further downhill now. When it wasn't working in the Edenic purity of Hydra it was hardly likely to do so in the staid environment of a city where deal-making was a priority and the sunlight of the island replaced by rain.

Cohen wasn't as attentive to Marianne in Montreal as he'd been in Hydra. At times she felt as if she had nothing more than an escapist holiday romance with him. Now it was back to cold reality. Her heart had no companion.

She liked his mother but she had too much free time on her hands when he was out. The job helped, but not enough. She wanted to go to university but her Norwegian grades didn't qualify her for this. She saw a new side to Cohen when he was with his friends, one she felt she could never be a part of. The magic of having him to herself in Hydra under the cerulean skies was a thing of the past.

Despite her free-spirited nature, Marianne was basically a one-man woman. She'd been like that with Jensen but he left her. Now history was repeating itself.

He pursued women like a heat-seeking missile. "My life was a blue movie," he admitted, "and blue movies are not romantic." It didn't matter; the time was with him. "I was very lucky," he crowed, "that my sexual appetites coincided with a period in history when young people were encouraged to indulge in untrammelled sexual congress.

She tolerated his infidelities in the hope that they'd burn themselves out but as time went on and more and more women threw themselves at him, that prospect seemed unlikely. "Everyone wanted a bit of my man," she lamented.[34]

She'd have been happy with him if he was a failed poet, a failed novelist, a failed anything. All she needed was love. But he was ambitious. That was the problem. She watched him drifting away from her to the world of executives, producers, deal makers.

It was no way to say goodbye.

From Page to Stage

Cohen intended to go to Nashville after he finished *Beautiful Losers* but instead became diverted to New York. There he encountered "the literati, the glitterati and the Warholian demi-monde."[1]

He knew he was heading into uncharted terrain when he turned his back on books. He became a singer, he said, because writing was so difficult. He needed to escape the horrors of the blank page.

He was going into a world where he probably wouldn't be accepted. At this time he was still the preserve of the culture vultures from Montreal's sophisticated set. It was difficult to imagine him creating a storm with the offbeat hippies that frequented places like Café Wha? in Greenwich Village to hear Bob Dylan warbling. He was more likely to have bespectacled introverts swooning to his rhythms in the fashionable bedsits of the suburbs.

Dylan almost single-handedly took him away from the worlds of Layton and Dudek. They feared such an environment could destroy Cohen's literary gift instead of amplifying it. Cohen didn't see it that way. "All my writing," he insisted, "has guitars behind it, even the novels."[2] "Phrases come with chord changes," he explained.[3]

Dudek castigated him for descending from the artistic pinnacle he'd occupied at McGill to a world of "mere entertainment."[4] The times they were a-changing.

Cohen didn't make any attempt to invade Dylan's world. How could he? Even though he was younger than him by some years, he'd already made his mark on the music scene while Cohen was finessing his poetic gifts.

He referred to Dylan as "the Picasso of song" but he didn't see himself as an imitator of him. "I was doing what he did before he was," he claimed, "though not as well." Allen Ginsberg alleged that Dylan blew everyone's mind except Cohen's.[5]

Layton said, "Leonard's no longer in the poetry game." "Never again," Harry Rasky declared, "would he be an unknown poet on a sun-baked island again."[6]

He didn't feel he had to justify himself to Layton or anyone else who bulleted ahead with their life in a single groove. He simply wanted to explore a different one. "The time is over," he pronounced, "when poets should sit on marble stairs with black capes."[7]

It was nice to be feted as a poet but he wanted bigger grapes – the lure of the greasepaint and the roar of the crowd. Poets weren't generally well known. But what if he could write songs in a poetic manner – would that be a way of combining his two gifts?

Cohen was like a rabbit in the headlights as he roamed around New York. Even though he was into his third decade, there was an innocence about him as he surveyed the music scene. He exuded a Dick Whittington vibe: the greenhorn in the Big Smoke.

One of the first people he contacted was the music manager Mary Martin. His cousin Robert Hershorn told him about her. Like Cohen, Hershorn was the son of a clothing manufacturer, He also shared his love of writing and was the editor of a literary magazine, *Exchange*. They became close friends over the years.

Cohen was impressed by the fact that Martin had worked with Bob Dylan's manager Albert Grossman. The fact that she was Canadian, and a woman, also helped. It was unusual for a woman to be a manager at the time.

One night he met the actress/singer/model Nico in Andy Warhol's club, La Dom. He thought she was the most beautiful woman he'd ever seen. She was accompanied by the then unknown Jackson

Browne. Cohen wanted to date her but she turned him down, saying he was too old for her.

She did, however, introduce him to Lou Reed. Cohen was amazed that Reed was familiar with his work. Reed said he loved *Beautiful Losers*, putting it on a par with William Burroughs' *Naked Lunch*. On the night in question he had a copy of *Flowers for Hitler* on him. He asked Cohen to sign it. Both men felt that they should have been more famous. They spent the evening, Cohen joked, assuring one another that they were unrecognised geniuses.

Nico was living with Browne at the time but would soon break up with him. She would go on to have romances with Jim Morrison and Jimi Hendrix, the two icons of rock. She was singing with the group Velvet Underground at the time. She'd even had a small part in Fellini's *La Dolce Vita*.

Cohen did all he could to get her interested in him, including wearing amulets and performing incantations, but nothing worked. Her singing was flat but mesmeric. She was said to sound like "an IBM computer with a German accent." Cohen went to see her night after night, sitting at her feet and staring at her like a misty-eyed teenager.[8]

He met Jack Kerouac at this time as well. It was on a night when he was reading his poetry to the backing of jazz musicians. Kerouac was sitting under a table at the time, pretending, as Cohen saw it, to be listening to the music.[9]

Kerouac was a legend at this time, like many of the Beat poets, but his talent was in decline. Cohen wasn't awed by the Beats. He'd met wilder people that nobody ever heard of or would hear of. Likewise with the outrageous rockers who sometimes stayed in the Chelsea Hotel. Janis Joplin and Mick Jagger were legends of sorts too. He admired them for what they did, despite it being light years away from his own style of singing. The same wasn't true for them. They saw him as someone who read poetry to old ladies from sewing circles.

Cohen fell between two stools. He was, as one writer put it, "too young to be a Beat and too old to be a folk singer."[10]

He didn't know any of the Beats well but he'd read their works. Ginsberg's "Howl" was perhaps the best-known Beat text. Ginsberg was close to Bob Dylan. Cohen had met Gregory Corso in Hydra. He was an admirer of William Burroughs as well.

Lou Reed may have seen a debt to him in *Beautiful Losers*. Cohen had also adopted some of Jack Kerouac's "junkyard prose" style when writing the book. He had a lot in common with Kerouac. Both of them were attached to their mothers, both of them were proficient in French and both of them devoted to Zen Buddhism.

Even though he wasn't cool enough for the Beats, he felt the chaotic state of his mind might appeal to the youth. In an interview in 1967 he said, "The thing people are interested in doing now is blowing their heads off. That's why the writing of schizophrenics like myself will be important to them."[11]

He didn't take his rejection by the Beats to heart. Maybe he didn't feel he had a right to be among them. He may have been a better writer than most of them but he wasn't living his art in the way they were.

He knew he appeared retrogressive to them. For one thing he dressed too well. And he was too polite. He needed more of an edge to him, an "attitude". They saw him as the type of man you could bring home to your mother. He didn't have a whiff of cordite.

His relationship to them, in any case, was peripheral now that he was considering leaving the printed page for the world of music.

His age was an even bigger problem. When he approached agents they said to him, "Aren't you a little old for this game?"[12] Deciding to become a pop singer at 33 in an era where young people were advised never to trust anyone over 30 was, to say the least, a bold move. There was also the question of his voice.

He never claimed to have much of a one, saying that if he had he wouldn't have started out as a writer. He would have sung other people's songs instead. Becoming a writer gave him the entitlement to sing his own ones.

"It has been conclusively established that I do not know how to sing," he said once, "but like the bumblebee who defies the law of aerodynamics, I persist."[13]

The first hurdle he'd have to overcome, Martin told him, was the obvious one of "poet turned singer." She knew he was going to be an easy target for that label and that it would be used to threaten his new ambition. An associated brickbat was the "difficulty" of his lyrics. They were hardly hit parade material.

She mentioned Cohen to her friend Judy Collins. She told her he was a novelist-cum-poet who read his poetry in clubs. Collins knew nothing about him at this time but upon Martin's recommendation she read his two novels and was entranced by them. When Cohen called to her house soon afterwards she was entranced by him too. Collins had been at the heart of the folk boom.

On the day they met he was supposed to sing his songs for her but instead they went to dinner. She wasn't sure if he was trying to seduce her or not. She saw him as smart and funny but also somewhat dangerous.[14]

He sang "Suzanne" for her the following day, introducing it by saying, "I can't sing and I can't play the guitar and I don't know if this is a song." After he finished it she said, "Well, you can sing and you can play the guitar a little and I'm recording that tomorrow."[15]

He also sang another song for her, "Dress Rehearsal Rag." It was about suicide. Collins had attempted to take her life years before so it had a particular resonance for her.

She decided to put both of the songs on her next album. Her ambition was to make it deeper than her previous ones.

A few weeks after Collins recorded "Suzanne," she invited Cohen to join her at a benefit she was doing. Jimi Hendrix was also going to be performing at it.

Cohen was terrified at the prospect of singing opposite the rock legend. As he prepared to go on, Collins noticed his legs shaking inside his trousers. He stuttered through a few verses of "Suzanne" before having a meltdown and walking offstage. He'd read his poetry in public on many occasions but this was different. He distrusted his singing voice.

The audience was quiet for a few moments after he went off. Then they started applauding. They wanted him back. Collins followed him to the side of the stage. "He looked about ten years old," she said. He was taking his guitar strap off. "I can't do it," he muttered. She touched him on the shoulder: "But you will," she assured him. She was right. He returned to the stage and finished the song. The audience went wild.[16]

Stories differ on why he had to leave the stage. Some said nerves; others said a broken string. Cohen told the audience. "Today my guitar is full of tears and feathers."[17] That impressed them more than any song could have. Such vulnerability became a large part of his attraction over the years for audiences. They grooved to the "little boy lost" aura he projected. "People love you when you fall apart," Collins reflected.

She didn't remember Cohen breaking a string. He said his guitar wasn't tuned. That would have added to his stage fright. Whatever the reason, the experience left him with mixed feelings about his future.

He wrote to Marianne afterwards, telling her it gave him "a curious kind of happiness" to have failed so spectacularly on his first major appearance. There was something beautiful about failure, he said, which made him "drunk." A part of him was relieved that his career had come to nothing. He ended by saying, "A cult may grow around this disaster."[18]

He advised Collins to start writing her own songs now. She hadn't thought of doing so before but soon afterwards she wrote one, appropriately titled "Since You Asked." It appeared on her next album, *Wildflowers*, along with three other Cohen numbers, 'Priests", 'Sisters of Mercy" and "Hey, That's No Way To Say Goodbye."

Martin was delighted things had gone so well with Collins. She told Cohen she was going to use his link with her as a springboard to try to get him a contract with Columbia records. She knew John Hammond, Columbia's talent scout.

Cohen began to see the positives from his collaboration with Collins. Up to now most of the main influences in his life were women – Masha, Esther, Marianne, Martin. Now another one had come along. What did that say about his personality? Was he, as the Americans said, "pussy-whipped?" Had his mother made him into a nebbish? He took solace from the fact that Bob Dylan's path to the big time had also been helped by a woman. Joan Baez was a bigger name than him when they started singing together.

Marianne was uneasy about the situation. She was so far away from him in Hydra. But he kept in touch with her regarding everything that was going on in his life when he was in the States. In April 1967 he wrote in a letter, "I put steel strings on my guitar. That's like changing from underwear to armour. Someone in Hollywood wants to buy "Suzanne." There are offers from Newport Folk Festival, a tour in the fall of forty American colleges."

He also addressed the problem of Axel. Neither of them knew what kind of future would be best for him now that the freewheeling sixties was coming to an end. Cohen advocated a radical solution to try and ground the young boy: "I can't help thinking that a New York slum is the best place for him, or if not that, a farm."

They eventually put him into a progressive school, Summerhill, in Suffolk, England. It was idealistic in its intent and in many ways before its time. Pupils didn't have to attend classes if they didn't feel like it. Cohen liked its freewheeling atmosphere. It reminded him of Hydra. But sometimes discipline was a good thing, especially for a young boy.

Marianne thought the school's *laissez-faire* system wouldn't suit Axel. She was right about that. There was some bullying as well. He wrote to her almost every day asking for her to take him out of it. She wanted to but she couldn't. This gave her tremendous guilt in the years afterwards.

"I put my life before his," she said, "I was always on the move. He suffered so much from my neglect of him."

Cohen appeared at Newport later that year with singers like Gordon Lightfoot and his fellow Canadian, Joni Mitchell. He made a big impression at it, becoming, in the words of one writer, "the high priest of a newly sanctified church dedicated to the art of lyrical seduction."[19]

He appeared again with Mitchell later that summer at the Mariposa Festival. At this time he helped her with her writing as well as her singing, encouraging her to "plumb the depths" of her experience when she sang.[20] He also encouraged her to draw, soliciting the advice of his friend Mort Rosengarten to set her on her way.

Cohen had a romantic relationship with her that went on for almost a year after the festival. The reasons for their parting weren't explained but she seemed upset by it, if the way she spoke about Cohen afterwards is anything to go by. She denounced him both as a writer and as a man. "He borrowed from Camus and Lorca" she said in one instance.

Mitchell made other snide digs at Cohen over the years. One time, she said, she painted a "really bad" portrait of him which she gave to a friend, "and their house burned down."[21] It's difficult to know what to make of a statement like this. It seems to have come from bitterness of some sort.

So Long, Marianne

Marianne went to New York that year but she didn't live with Cohen. Instead she stayed with a friend in an apartment in New York. He, meanwhile, decamped at the famous Chelsea Hotel. She started to hear his songs on the radio, songs that were once sung to her alone, songs he'd serenaded her with. They were now being shared with the world.

The hotel was rich in musical and literary lore. It was where Bob Dylan wrote "Sad-Eyed Lady of the Lowlands." Where Arthur C. Clarke wrote *2001: A Space Odyssey*. Where William Burroughs wrote *Naked Lunch* and where Arthur Miller wrote *After The Fall*. It was also a place where tragedies took place, like the killing of Nancy Spungeon by Sid Vicious. Dylan Thomas went into the coma that finally saw him "go gentle into the good night" in the hotel.

Cohen ran into Janis Joplin one day in an elevator there. He told her he was looking for Brigitte Bardot. She said she was looking for Kris Kristofferson.

"You're in luck," he announced, "I'm Kris Kristofferson!" It was a measure of her desperation, he remarked, that she actually believed him for a few seconds. It hasn't been documented if she said she was Brigitte Bardot. What we know for sure was that they ended up in bed together, each of them the other's second best.

Cohen later wrote a song about their encounter, "Chelsea Hotel #2. "I wrote it," he claimed, "outside a Polynesian restaurant in Miami during a dismal period in my life while waiting for some spare ribs and a Thai cocktail." He regretted writing it because – uncharacteristically for him – it portrayed an identifiable person in a poor light. At the beginning, as most people now know, Joplin is described as performing fellatio on him. "She wouldn't have minded," he said, " but my mother would."[1]

Joplin once said, "I make love to 25,000 people on stage and then come home alone." Cohen often saw her wandering around hotel rooms looking for someone to talk to.

She stood for something "beautiful and nervous and high," he said, and "surrendered completely" to people in her life.[2] Maybe that was her undoing. Three years later she overdosed, having recorded Kristofferson's song "Me and Bobby McGee" just three days before she died. Kristofferson couldn't listen to the song afterwards without breaking down.

Cohen introduced Marianne to Joplin, and also to people like Andy Warhol and Buffy Sainte-Marie. She was out of her depth in such company. Cohen revelled in it. Marianne knew they were going in opposite directions fast.

Sainte-Marie was a big admirer of Cohen's songwriting, saying it was so diverse it reminded her of going from Times Square to the Bronx Zoo. Marianne couldn't engage in these kinds of conversations. They were anathema to her. He took her to a Joplin concert one night which didn't mean anything to her either.

Marianne's apartment was on Clinton Street. She was staying there with Axel and a university student called Carol Zemel. Every morning Zemel went off to the campus and Axel to school. Marianne designed handcrafts which she sold on the streets. Cohen told her it was dangerous to do that. She was robbed one day at knife-point. She felt nostalgic for Hydra, where she'd been "barefoot, poor and in love."[3] She was still in love – and poor. Cohen paid her half of the rent.

Marianne slept with men to try and get her mind off Cohen. One of them was a photographer she'd met in Hydra, Jean-Marc Appert. Cohen's Burberry coat was stolen from the apartment one night. He suspected Appert was the culprit. He wrote "Famous Blue Raincoat" around this time.

Zemel believed she had a hand in the composition of the song. Her ex-husband lived in the Arizona desert. Cohen wrote to him one night in the apartment as Zemel lay sleeping. When she woke up he told her about the letter. She said, "Give him my regards."

The references to sleeping, the desert, and the "regards" all link her to the song, as of course does the address of Clinton Street.[4] The line, "Did you ever go clear?" is said to be a reference to Scientology, a movement Cohen was flirting with at this time.

His career started to take off in earnest now. John Hammond told Mary Martin he was interested in listening to him after hearing Judy Collins singing his songs. Hammond had already signed people like Billie Holiday, Aretha Franklin and Bob Dylan. He had a reputation for taking chances. When Dylan's first album flopped, it became known as "Hammond's Folly" for a time.

Cohen played a selection of his songs for Hammond one night. He couldn't tell by his expression whether he was enjoying them or not. When Cohen was finished, he said to him, "You've got it." Cohen didn't know what "it" meant. Was it a contract or the more abstract quality of "talent"? He said afterwards they were the three best words he'd ever heard.[5]

Hammond told him he'd like to sign him but would have to get the approval of his colleagues first. Walter Yetnikoff was running Columbia at this time. When he met Cohen he's alleged to have uttered the now classic phrase, "We know you're great, Leonard, but are you any good?"[6] Cohen was left scratching his head at the left-handed compliment as Yetnikoff reluctantly agreed to take him on.

The sarcasm was characteristic of him. What he was saying in effect was that he wasn't buying the sense of awe that surrounded Cohen in some quarters. Such a feeling would persist with him right through Cohen's involvement with Columbia.

Martin now introduced him to a music publisher called Jeff Chase. She thought he might be able to advance his career. They worked together on a demo tape of some of his songs but clashed on the finer points of their arrangement. Before they started, Chase had insisted Cohen sign a document giving him rights over three of the songs they were recording, "Suzanne," "Dress Rehearsal Rag" and "Master Song."

When Cohen decided to walk away from the recording session, Chase said he was going to keep the publishing rights to the songs to compensate him for his wasted time. Cohen was shocked. He asked Martin what he should do. Bizarrely, she advised him to accede to Chase's demand. The only saving grace was that he'd only given publishing rights to his material to Chase, not performing ones. He still retained these.

Another man Cohen met at this time was the producer Bob Johnston. He'd made albums with Dylan, Johnny Cash and Simon and Garfunkel. Cohen told him about the Jeff Chase debacle. Johnston was shocked at Martin's accession to his demands. He advised Cohen to get rid of her, telling him he'd be his producer now if he was interested. Cohen was. Johnston also introduced Cohen to a lawyer, Marty Machat, whom Cohen went on to employ in that capacity.

He now recorded his first album, *Songs of Leonard Cohen*. It was a different kind of sound to what was generally played on the airwaves. Hammond was reputed to have said, "Watch out, Dylan!" as his new recruit sang his first words. They were rich. The public weren't going to get a "moon in June" rhyming scheme, or speculations about someone down at the five-and-dime worrying about chewing gum losing its flavour on the bedpost overnight.

Hammond became ill as the recording went on so he handed Cohen over to his associate, John Simon. Cohen didn't like Simon's arrangement of his songs. He wanted to add drums to "Suzanne," for instance. Cohen thought that would "push it into the area of popular music," something he was determined not to do.

Simon had been in favour of a more elaborate production in other ways as well. Cohen was never interested in the "bells and whistles" approach to music. He distanced himself from Simon, who ended up leaving him to his own devices. He would be less successful a decade later during a similar disagreement with Phil Spector.

Nobody knew what to make of Cohen at this point. He was said to have the face of a "benign undertaker" and to sing like a "sad troubadour" who wanted women to mother him.

His lyrics seemed to be coming from a cathedral, lyrics sharpened to within an inch of their lives. Emotions were rubbed raw in the sandpaper of his heart. His singing, one commentator wrote, was "as calm as a pond and as strange as a séance."[7]

He wasn't the type of singer you listened to if you were with somebody, even if he gave the promise of that somebody. It was music for lonely hearts, or broken ones, or both. Especially female ones. He told women there was someone out there who understood what they were going through, someone who could put a balm over the wound – because he'd been that soldier.

Reaction to the album was mixed. People asked, "Who is this guy? Where had he been? Nobody was too surprised to hear he was a poet before becoming a singer. It was unusual for somebody contemplating a musical career to be receiving poetry awards from universities. His stints at coffeehouses were regarded as footnotes to his other life rather than vice versa.

The set list was "Suzanne," "The Stranger Song," "Hey, That's No Way to Say Goodbye," "Master Song," "Sisters of Mercy," "Stories of the Street," "Winter Lady" "So Long, Marianne" and "Teachers." His tremolo style of guitar playing was more evident in 'The Stranger Song" than any of his other ones. It was what he'd learned from his ill-fated flamenco teacher.

People wanted to know where such evocative songs came from. Were they based on fact or his imagination? 'So Long, Marianne," one writer said, was "as beautiful a 'Dear John' letter as there ever was."

He'd written "Sisters of Mercy" on a night when he was in Edmonton, sheltering from a snowstorm in an alcove. Two pretty girls were there with backpacks. When he started talking to them, it emerged that they had nowhere to stay so he invited them back to his hotel room. He admitted to having fantasies of sexual congress with them but as soon as they got inside the door they fell onto his bed and were asleep in an instant.

They looked so innocent he promptly gave up any ideas he may have had of seducing either of them, or both. Instead he sat into an armchair and looked out at the night. There was a full moon over the frozen Saskatchewan river. It inspired him to write a song. He took up his guitar and started singing the words softly to himself. Before he knew it, the song was done. He'd never composed one that quickly before, or one that didn't have to be changed in any way. This was more like the way Bob Dylan wrote. When the girls woke up he sang it to them. It was a perfect night, a perfect song, a perfect relationship. This was the spiritual Cohen, not the sexually-charged one. There's even a Catholic pun in the title. He could change from one guise to another when the occasion demanded.

Most of the talk was about "Suzanne," the song that opened the album. People wanted to know who she was. In future years she'd be confused with the "other" Suzanne in his life, the one who bore him two children.

For now there was only one lady with that name: Suzanne Verdal. The song had appeared as a poem in his book *Parasites of Heaven*. It also contained another poem attesting to her beauty, 'Suzanne Wears a Leather Coat." This described how such beauty caused the traffic to stop when she walked across the street.

Verdal was a dancer and choreographer. She'd been married to a sculptor called Armand Villaincourt but was now separated from him. When Cohen met her she was renting an apartment on the Saint Lawrence river in a part of Montreal that had a harbour with a statue of Our Lady on it. She didn't actually serve him tea and oranges as such, rather tea with bits of orange peel in it, but "tea and oranges," he said, sounded better.[8]

'Suzanne" showed Cohen's facility with combining Jewish and Christian imagery in the same way as he would conflate Judaism with Zen Buddhism in future years. He didn't like boundaries. By definition they were limiting – to both his literary vision and his intellectual stances.

He liked using Biblical allusions in his songs, not only because of their profound overtones, but because he knew there was a good chance people would pick up on them. He was "tapping into a common reservoir." [9]

She wasn't one of his lovers, merely a friend. He made a pass at her once, she claimed, but she rebuffed him.[10] He was relieved about this afterwards. It would, he said, have destroyed the purity of the song if they had an affair. He touched her body with his mind in it "because there was no other opportunity."[11]

Verdal said she thought Cohen should have given her some of the royalties from "Suzanne." This was a strange request. Cohen didn't think he should, even if she gave him the idea for the song. It's hard to disagree with him.

On this line of reasoning, there are millions of people out there who deserve royalties from singers. But Cohen was the type of man one could imagine giving an *ex gratia* payment for such courtesies even if these hadn't been compromised by Jeff Chase. Maybe he would have if their relationship was closer.

Cohen's friends told him they loved the album, that it laid the groundwork for a career. His threnodies of lament captured their hearts. He appreciated their approval but he wasn't sure his move from literature to music was secure yet. He may have been a household name now but outside the recording studio he found himself "walking the streets trying to find someone to have a cup of coffee with."

That was probably because of the lack of any identifiable image of himself that he was perpetrating. The cover image of him reminded one listener of the "long-dead hero of some forgotten south American revolution rather than something you could relate to the world of

The Tremeloes or the first sighting of Jimi Hendrix on "The Lulu Show."[12]

Cohen set out his stall as a "woman's singer" with the album. Four of the tracks referenced women in the titles ("Suzanne," "Winter Lady" "Sisters of Mercy" and "So Long, Marianne") and many others in their lyrics. Women would soon become his main audience too – and his focus even when he wasn't singing about (or to) them.

He became depressed after the album went on release. It took so much out of him he wasn't sure he wanted to continue being a singer. He met Bob Johnston at a party one night in L.A. Johnston told him he needed to get away. "Why not go to Nashville?" he said.

It had been his intended pitstop before he got diverted to New York. He thought it sounded like a good idea to go there now. Johnston told him he could cut his next album there if he wanted. It would jibe with his love of country music. Johnston had some session musicians he knew working there, Ron Cornelius (who would go on to write a book about working with Cohen) and the then-unknown Charlie Daniels.

He liked the idea of getting back to nature. Bob Dylan had "gone country" after his 1966 motorcycle crash and produced *John Wesley Harding* and *Nashville Skyline.*

Cohen wondered where he'd stay if he agreed to Johnston's suggestion. Johnston said he had a friend with the unlikely name of Boudleaux Bryant. Bryant had written the Everly Brothers hit, "Bye Bye, Love." He owned a farm outside a town called Franklin. Johnston felt sure Cohen would be welcome to stay there.

The rent was only $40 a month. That sealed the deal for him. He decided to make the long delayed trip. As soon as he got there he already felt at home.

This was a time he remembered fondly. It was fulfilling to him in a different way to the elemental Hydra. He liked looking at the wild pea-fowl outside his door. In the winter there were icicles. He had fun firing bullets at them with a rifle he bought from an army surplus store. (His fondness for firearms isn't too well-known. He was even a member of the NRA).

The farm extended over 2000 acres. It was 35 miles from Nashville. Cohen's nearest neighbour, a toothless moonshiner who'd served time in prison for killing a sheriff in the forties, lived half a mile away. Cohen found him to be pleasant company anytime they met.

In his book *The Guitar Behind Dylan and Cohen*, Cornelius recounted meeting Cohen for the first time. He was "buck naked" on that occasion, he recollected.

The pair of them often drank with Willie York, the toothless moonshiner, and a rodeo star called Kid Marley. Cohen, according to Cornelius, was "out of sorts" most of the time but "loving every minute of it." Marley once sold Cohen a lame horse, something that became a source of great amusement to him.

Cohen recorded his second album in Nashville. It has a country influence, but not as much as one might have expected considering his living conditions when he made it. He was uncomfortable in this new environment and deferred to Johnston for guidance in how to handle it. How could the arid plains of Tennessee inspire him like the blue seas of the Aegean did?

If *Beautiful Losers* showed signs of "that difficult second novel," *Songs From a Room* did likewise with that "difficult second album." It had brilliant elements in it but for the public the surprise factor was gone. Cohen was known now – for his voice, his orientation, his poetry, his delivery. The long knives could have been expected to come out.

Austerity, as the album's title indicates, was its keynote. The cover became iconic. It showed a bare room, a table, a pretty blonde woman wrapped in a towel sitting on a chair in front of a typewriter. What else could a writer need for inspiration? This, of course, was Marianne. But it was a false sell as Cohen and Marianne had split up by now.

Nonetheless, the stand-out number on the album was the one she inspired, "Bird on the Wire," just like the stand-out number on his previous one was inspired by Suzanne Verdal.

The other songs on it were lower profile: the semi-political, semi-Biblical "Story of Isaac," "A Bunch of Lonesome Heroes" (which, again, came from one of his poems), "The Partisan," a song about the French Resistance during World War II which he didn't write himself, and two decidedly obscure songs, "The Old Revolution" and "The Butcher." He seemed on more comfortable ground with the intimate songs dealing with his relationships with women: "You Know Who I am," "Lady Midnight," "Tonight Will Be Fine."

The album came out the same year as The Beatles' *Sergeant Pepper's Lonely Hearts Club Band*. That suited the time more than Cohen's meditative ramblings. It was an era when kipper ties and Union Jack underpants were about to yield to floral bandannas and one's first acid trip.[13]

Where was Cohen going to fit into this algorithm? Was he going to be "last year's man" – to coin a phrase?

Songs From a Room had many songs centred around the theme of death. One of them, "Seems So Long Ago, Nancy," dealt with a 21-year old woman who shot herself after an illegitimate baby she'd given birth to was taken from her. Contemporary listeners found it difficult to believe such things could happen. Cohen was a little older than them. He had experience of such a world. His friend Nancy Chailles died by her own hand, shooting herself in her bathroom in Montreal in the mid-sixties as a result of the depression she underwent after losing her child.

People either loved or hated the album. Cohen became a marker not only for music but the kind of people one wanted to hang out with. Suzanne Vega said if she asked someone if they liked him and they said, "Who?" she knew immediately that she couldn't be their friend.[14] She believed that being a fan of Cohen was like being part of a "secret society."

The decade ended with some seismic events, both euphoric and horrific. Neil Armstrong walked on the moon. Charles Manson butchered Sharon Tate and her friends. Films like Easy Rider and rock festivals like Woodstock ushered in a new way of living.

Cohen wasn't the type of person to link movements with eras. He just lurched from day to day. The sixties, he once said, lasted "maybe fifteen or twenty minutes in somebody's mind."[15] He saw it as a fabrication of sociologists to suggest a mindset, an orientation.

He was never going to give himself over to the shibboleths of flower power or free love so it was really a forgettable decade for him. Maybe he said this because he was in Hydra when all the madness was going on in America during the decade. If you can remember the sixties, as they say, you weren't there.

Marianne must have wondered what she was doing on the sleeve of his album. It was good of her to allow him put her there. She went back to Norway now, finally having accepted the fact that he was gone from her. He didn't sell the house on Hydra, telling her she could go back to it any time she wanted, but he couldn't stay with her there anymore. "I wanted many women," he declared, "many kinds of experiences, many countries, many climates, many love affairs."[16]

Their relationship fizzled out "like ashes falling." There were no heated arguments, no soul-searchings. It simply ran its course, lasting somewhat longer than the sixties "fifteen minutes" but in a sense epitomising the bohemianism the decade enunciated. It was time to wake up from that Edenic glow now, time to gird one's lions for the consumerist decade to come.

They weren't the only couple waking up. George Johnston and Charmian Clift went back to Sydney after Johnston contracted tuberculosis.

Charmian committed suicide in 1969. Johnstown died the following year. In 1974 their son Shane also killed himself. Another son, Martin, became an alcoholic and died in his early forties.

Axel's situation worsened with time. Jensen took him to India when he was 15 and gave him LSD while he was there. Axel couldn't handle this, or his peripatetic lifestyle. He eventually developed psychological problems that resulted in him having to be institutionalised in Norway. Jensen continued to write and to have relationships with different women. In his later life he contracted a muscular disease that paralyzed him. Cohen paid for his hospitalisation.

Marianne took up painting and Buddhism and wrote her autobiography. In it she told her co-writer, Kari Hesthamar, how guilty she felt about Axel. Her own life had been too chaotic for her to be a proper mother to him as he grew up. It was wrong of her to pack him off to Summerhill. And of course it was wrong of Jensen to give him LSD. He never really recovered from either experience.

The dream had ended for all of them. Cohen's hero W.B. Yeats wrote, "Things fall apart. The centre cannot hold."

Cohen put it a different way. "Once you've lived in Hydra," he said, "you can never live anywhere else – including Hydra."

Famous Blue Leonard

As all these things were happening around him, Cohen met two people who were about to become huge in his life: Suzanne Elrod, who would give birth to two children by him, and Joshu Sasaki Roshi, a Japanese Zen Master to whom he became a personal assistant. Each of them fulfilled a different side to him but also tried his patience to its limit. Barrie Wexler believed Cohen found in Roshi the kind of bonding he never had with a woman.

The duties he was expected to perform for him were cook, driver and drinking companion – not necessarily in that order. From his anecdotes about their time together, maybe the third of these ranked highest for the mercurial monk.

Cohen told an interviewer once that he was never interested in Zen Buddhism. What he was interested in was Roshi. He was amazed at his ability to be so at home in the world when he himself wasn't at home anywhere. If Roshi had been a professor of Physics at Heidelberg university, he told the interviewer, he would have followed him there instead of to his centre.[1]

Roshi was no ordinary monk. He liked alcohol, for instance, and sex. He also had many scary mood swings, foaming at the mouth when he became annoyed and rocking rooms when he laughed. He was anything but spiritual in many of his pronouncements. He once said, "You can't live in paradise. No restaurants or toilets."

Suzanne Elrod fascinated Cohen in a different way. She was as unpredictable as Roshi and somewhat more attractive physically.

The first time he saw her was at a Scientology seminar. It was in an elevator. She was coming out and he going in. A few days later he saw her again when she was bending over a desk signing a registration form. He apparently said to his Zen friend Eric Lerner, "You know how short women's skirts were in those days. I was completely captivated by the sight of her ass. I didn't even see her face."² This is an unlikely revelation from a man more usually associated with extolling the merits of women's inner beauty but Lerner insisted it happened.

Part of his attraction to her, he said later, sprang from the fact that her name was the same as that of the eponymous character of his most famous song. One writer contended that this wasn't strictly speaking true, that Elrod's birth name was Susan, not Suzanne, and that she changed it after meeting Cohen.³

She was living with another man at the time. She left him for Cohen. As was the case with Marianne, she felt she was meant to be with him. The man she'd been living with insisted on meeting him. He was so impressed with Cohen that he bought his books and records afterwards, telling Elrod he didn't feel so bad losing her when he saw how impressive his replacement was.

Cohen was now about to add a new string to his bow by taking the album on tour. This was Columbia's decision rather than his. He always liked travelling but not when it involved work, or when someone else chose the destinations.

At first he didn't want to do the tour. He dug his heels in, saying he wouldn't do it. "How are we going to sell the album then?" the Columbia bosses enquired.

He said they should have set up a marketing campaign for it. They didn't like doing that, imagining he had only a niche following. He felt it was all a vicious circle. Money created sales and sales created money. Who was going to blink first?

He didn't enjoy tours in those days, seeing them as necessary evils of his trade. Writing was his first love and singing his second. Making a living out of that was the hard part. Going on tour, in his view, was huckstering. It was a way of saying to audiences, "Buy my album" over an indeterminate number of nights where he would do the same *shtick*.

There was also the fear that a performance wouldn't go well. He was insecure in these early days of his career. In a studio, one could cover over a bad dub with another one. Concerts didn't provide the same escape hatch. It was like the difference between theatre and film acting. In those days he didn't have the confidence to send himself up, or be indifferent to public appraisals of him.

The tour began in Amsterdam and continued on to the Isle of Wight. He appeared in a controversial festival there. There were over 600,000 people at it. The crowd were restless. Shortly beforehand they'd set fire to a food stand. Cohen was scheduled to come on at midnight but things got delayed. He fell asleep in his trailer waiting for his slot. That turned out to be at four in the morning.

He had to be woken up to do his set. When he stepped on stage at first he was wearing a raincoat. Before singing "Bird on the Wire" he kept saying, "I wrote this for Marianne, I wrote this for Marianne. I hope she's here. I hope she's here." His eyes looked dead. He was obviously "out of it."

The audience had been aggressive with performers who'd come on before him. They heckled Joan Baez, threw bottles at Kris Kristofferson and burned the stage when Hendrix came on. Kristofferson was so disgusted by the reception accorded to his rendition of "Me and Bobby McGee" that he gave a middle finger to

65

the crowd before him, who didn't appreciate the gesture and let him know it.

Cohen was expecting them to turn on him too but he managed to pacify them somehow, his gentle strains making the vast venue seem like a hermetically sealed boudoir. He introduced "Suzanne" by saying, "Maybe this is good music to make love to". A comment like that was always going to go down well with young people shaking off the constraints of the previous generation.

He won them over further by beseeching them all to light matches so he could see them. In this he was before his time. It's now commonplace for audiences to light candles at open air concerts but nothing like this had been done in 1970. The gesture pacified them. It made them feel the kind of intimacy no Cohen concert should be without.

Kristofferson was mesmerised at the change in them, especially after Cohen had taken, as he put it, "twenty minutes" to tune up. "Then he did the damnedest thing you ever saw," he recalled, "He charmed the beast. A lone sorrowful voice did what some of the best rockers in the world had tried to do and failed."[4] This was the night, one could say, that Cohen first manifested his magnetic stage persona.

It was one of Hendrix' last concerts. Three weeks later he was dead, choking on his vomit in a hotel room. Hendrix and Janis Joplin died within a fortnight of one another that year, both checking out from overdoses at the same age (27) on September 18 and October 4 respectively. Cohen was getting a baptism by fire into what the path of excess led to. It wasn't, as William Blake imagined, a palace of wisdom.

He did a concert in London towards the end of the year in which he was high himself. He began his set with a mock-Nazi salute, thereafter drinking a toast to the memories of both Hendrix and Joplin. At a party afterwards he behaved bizarrely. One person at it remarked, "Everyone was waiting for him to levitate."[5]

Part of his erratic behaviour probably resulted from relief. It was his first time really testing himself with the public after his panic attack at the Judy Collins show. If he was going to be serious about a career in music he had to get over this hurdle. The stakes were too high. "Performing," he announced, "is an opportunity for a thousand humiliations." Especially when he knew he was going to be written about afterwards.

Irving Layton's wife Aviva said he took reviews of his concerts seriously even when they were printed in small publications. One day she saw him in his dressing room writing to a Montreal newspaper in response to a poor review of one of his concerts there. "Why do you bother?" she said to him, *The London Star* says you're great. *The New York Times* says you're fantastic. You get international rave reviews. Why do you care what the pathetic little *Montreal Star* writes?" He replied, "My mother reads it. She's convinced I'm a failure."[6]

Avril Giacobbi was doing PR for Bob Johnston at this time. She met Cohen backstage at the Royal Albert Hall before a London concert. She told him she was organising a press conference for him the following day.

"I've never been to a press conference," he wailed, "I can't do it." She was amazed that such a well-known entertainer could be so nervous. The concert was a success but he was unhappy with the reserve of British audiences.

67

"They didn't like me," he insisted, pacing up and down the dressing room floor, "cancel the press." She had to remind him that he'd got a standing ovation after one of his songs.[7]

He had an ambivalent attitude to his growing recognition. Did he really want it, he wondered. Fame meant taxis and aeroplanes and living like a vampire in a recording studio. "When you're mixing a record," he complained, "you never see the sunlight."[8] Concerts brought different kinds of pressure – an excess of visibility.

He was often mistaken for Al Pacino or Dustin Hoffman. In 1970 he was congratulated by five people for the fine performance he'd given in the film *Midnight Cowboy*. Asked by a tourist if he was a famous actor he replied, "No. I'm a famous nobody."

The 1971 release *McCabe and Mrs Miller,* directed by Robert Altman, featured three songs from his first album on the soundtrack, "The Stranger Song," "Sisters of Mercy" and "Winter Lady." Cohen liked Altman. He talked to him about his film *Brewster McCloud* rather than the more high profile *M*A*S*H* (which he hadn't seen) and was happy to allow him use the songs.

In his contract with him he added a codicil stipulating that Altman receive a percentage of any earnings his *Songs of Leonard Cohen* album made after the film's release. It was a typically gentlemanly attitude which he showed to people right through his life. Altman was touched by it. He'd never experienced that kind of benevolence in anyone in business before.

Cohen didn't like Altman's film the first time he saw it. The songs hadn't been included at this stage. Altman was devastated. When he saw it again with the songs in it he loved it. Altman was relieved but the film didn't do well for him. It was admired for Cohen's songs but not for anything else. An atmospheric turn-of-the-century piece, it didn't do well at the box office, despite starring Warren Beatty and Julie Christie. They were "hot" at the time but became suffocated under Altman's moody indulgences.

Cohen was now ready to make his third album. It would prove to be one of his most controversial. Like *Songs From a Room*, he recorded *Songs of Love and Hate* in Tennessee with Bob Johnston. It contained many dark songs but also many poetic ones, especially "Famous Blue Raincoat," which would become a kind of signature tune for him in time.

He didn't think much of it himself. It's unclear why. He said he thought the "carpentry" showed. Few people agreed, seeing it as one of his most evocative compositions. Many people have tried to figure out what its about over the years. All we know for sure is that it concerns a love triangle being discussed in a letter. But who is the letter about? Or to? One writer even deduced that it was written from Cohen to himself.[9]

Cohen said he didn't understand the song either. Was this a ploy to avoid having to identify the actual people in it? Identifying Janis Joplin in "Chelsea Hotel" would backfire on him some years down the road. He said he wrote "Famous Blue Raincoat" with the idea of an "invisible male" seducing the woman he's currently living with in the song but even this he wasn't sure of.

He agreed that he himself may have been this male. Or even that it could have been a female.[10]

All of these speculations are ultimately futile, like speculations about any work of art. The bottom line is that the song means anything we want it to mean. What lingers in the mind is its imagery – the coat, the music on Clinton Street, the house in the desert, the rose in the teeth. And the main character, whoever he (or she) is, waiting forlornly for Lili Marlene at the train station.

The way Cohen signs off in the song ("Sincerely, L. Cohen") also confused people. Some listeners who didn't know him thought he might be Spanish, that the "L" was actually "El." When he heard this he changed the end to "Sincerely, A Friend." That lessened its impact considerably. (In 1991, a musical revue called "Sincerely, A Friend," based on Cohen's songs, was launched by the playwright Bryden MacDonald).

The cold formality of "Sincerely, L. Cohen" is surprising considering the emotionalism of what's gone before. One writer thought it was reminiscent of the "I don't even think of you that often" at the end of "Chelsea Hotel."[11]

Such off-handedness was telegraphed by many of the earlier lines in that song so to that extent it was acceptable. Here it goes against the grain of the foregoing intimacies.

"Last Year's Man" was also on the album. This was a song, he said, that he used to play on a Mexican guitar until he broke it one day by jumping on it "in a fit of impotent fury" in 1967.[12] He didn't say what caused the fury.

Songs of Love and Hate was generally regarded as Cohen's most dismal album to date – and it had some competition in that department. Three of the tracks ("Last Year's Man,," "Avalanche" and "Dress Rehearsal Rag") had suicide themes. These were hardly to propel it to the top of the hit parade.

Cohen fans, on the contrary, "forgave" him for such emphases because of their power. And for the power of some of the other numbers, like 'Joan of Arc" and 'Love Calls You By Your Name." Nick Cave was taken by "the trance-like picking of the guitar, the brutal black and white cover."[13]   It flopped in the U.S. That was partly due to Cohen's unwillingness to tour with it – a familiar problem.

Its failure dragged down his spirits. "I began to believe all the negative things people were saying about my singing", he grieved, "I began to hate the sound of my voice." [14]

He said to Marty Machat, "I can't sing." Machat replied, "None of you guys are able to sing. If I want to hear singers I go to the Metropolitan Opera".[15]   All Cohen could do was laugh at the insult. Even if he hadn't a great voice by conventional standards he felt he could make up for that by "living" his songs in the same way as Method actors were said to "live" their parts.

The album renewed all the old chestnuts about him being a depressing performer. After hearing it, a listener is alleged to have snorted, "Thank God Sylvia Plath never learned to sing!" The Irish writer Marianne Keyes sniped, "To have faith in something, to be happy, that's what most people want, isn't it? With the possible exception of Leonard Cohen."

The fact that Cohen dressed in dark clothes (grey or black usually) added to the vview in many people's minds that he was a sad sack. Having an image of being the "man in grey" (echoing Johnny Cash's "the man in black") caused his friend Earl Gordon to say to him one day, "You never have to worry about what you're going to wear the next day, do you?"[16]   Joan Baez referred to him as the "king of black predictions" and the "harbinger of a scorched earth." [17]

Another reason he was tagged with being depressing was the fact that his voice was so deep. He admitted it could sound "rather whiney". But to dismiss the songs as being summarily dismal on this account was to misrepresent them – and him.

The dark overtones, from this point of view, came not so much from the lyrics as their delivery. Cohen said it was just a "biological accident" that they sounded melancholy when he sang them.[18] That becomes clear when we listen to Judy Collins' versions of them, or anyone else who covered them throughout his career.

It should also be mentioned that Cohen had a horror of "happy clappy" songs like Louis Armstrong's "What a Wonderful World". These didn't reflect his experience. A pessimist, he said, was someone who was "waiting for it to rain" whereas he felt "drenched to the skin" by life.[19]

The denunciation of him wasn't shared by all his listeners. He once received a letter from a girl in Germany who said his songs gave great comfort to a friend of hers who was dying of cancer. The letter, he said, was "one of the most touching things I've ever read."

Cohen once told his friend Niema Ash that depressed people sometimes rang him telling him they were going to kill themselves and wanted his voice to be the last one they heard. She said he told her this not as a boast but in bewilderment.[20]

He believed "our sweetest songs" sometimes came from "saddest thoughts." There's often a beauty in melancholy. "We never say of a blues singer that he sounds sad," he pointed out.[21] That's because the emotion was inbuilt into the genre. As indeed it often was to country music. Somebody once joked that if you played a country music song backwards, you got a character who gave up drink, his wife cancelled the divorce she was planning and his dog came back from the grave.

Negative feelings, it should be added, never gave Cohen raw material for his songs. In fact they got in the way of it. The very fact of writing, of putting a "stain on the silence" to use Samuel Beckett's phrase, was proof that one was coming out of a bad place. Songwriting, like literature, was a form of catharsis.

Neither did Cohen make any apology for looking serious on stage. "A bullfighter doesn't enter the ring laughing," he noted. He was too busy worrying about whether he was going to live or die. A singer could "die" too – metaphorically speaking – if an audience didn't like him.

Marty Machat persuaded him to tour with the album. He began with a gig in Dublin's National Stadium in March 1972. Machat hired a film maker called Tony Palmer to make a documentary of the tour. It took in twenty cities in little more than a month.

Palmer was an accomplished filmmaker with a proven track record. He'd previously produced works with The Beatles, Cream and Frank Zappa as well as many other celebrities outside music. He was granted the kind of access to Cohen that would be unimaginable today during the shoot. That meant we got a warts 'n all film. Cohen looks exhausted for a lot of it – perhaps not surprisingly. Who could "do" twenty cities in a month without becoming exhausted?

His personality is also more outgoing in it than one might have expected. Was he "on" something? The manner in which he jokes with audiences (at one stage giving out to them for "recognising" a song he's about to play), or "does a Dylan" with interviewers, suggests he was. Asked by one interviewer what he'd like to talk about, he replies, "I prefer not to speak at all".

Elsewhere he says he can't sing, saying to the audience, "I think something is wrong every time you applaud". Of "Suzanne" he says, "Fortunately, the rights of this song were stolen from me. It would be wrong to get rich from it." A piece of paper was presented to him as a standard contract, he says, and the song was gone, just like that. The audience applauds.

Cohen hadn't looked forward to the idea of the film any more than he did to the idea of the tour, agreeing to both reluctantly in the hope that they'd advance his profile.

Was that profile his real self in the film or one he "adopted" in the interests of trying to be a court jester? It's hard to tell. At times he sings the songs as we expect him to. At other times he shouts out the lines as if he's trying to be Mick Jagger.

One scene has him shaving – without soap – to try and inspire himself for a return to the stage. Another has him flirting with a pretty woman who approaches after a concert with a suggested assignation. Palmer lets the camera run from behind his shoulder as he gently tries to tell her another time would be more appropriate. This is *cinema verité* at its best. We're getting a backstage pass into the kind of dressing room badinage only roadies would usually be privy to.

"I'm tough," he says at another point, "I can take it". But one wonders. Has "the road" been too arduous for him? Singing the same songs too often, he announces to the audience at one concert, makes them "inhospitable". A singer is left "banging at the door" if he loses contact with their emotion. That's one of the occupational hazards of touring.

The film begins with a concert in Tel Aviv where aggressive security guards fail to quell a disgruntled audience, leading to Cohen inviting them onto the stage with him where they'll be removed from such aggression. The idea of something like this happening today would be unthinkable, as would the prospect of a singer offering audience members their money back when they express dissatisfaction at the sound quality after a monitor malfunctions. That's what makes this such a treasurable piece of film. Unfortunately, however, Cohen didn't see it this way at the time, feeling he'd revealed too much of himself in it. (We can say this in all senses: One scene has him swimming naked in a hotel pool). "Tony, it's been wonderful," he says to Palmer at the end but he's speaking tongue in cheek.

He insisted on re-editing it, which meant it wasn't shown to the public until two years later, and even then in an unfinished form. It would be all of 36 years more before it was distributed in a manner that satisfied him.

Offstage, life was going well for him now. He was happy with Elrod. A stream gurgled outside their door. Birds and animals made similarly pleasing sounds. Cohen imitated them at night with friends when he was tipsy. He spoke of marrying Elrod, even giving her a ring at one point, but didn't take things any further.

"We admired the wild peacocks," Elrod recalled, "and listened to the stream in the morning. We watched the sunset in the evening." She was utterly devoted to Cohen at this time. "As long as someone like him was in the universe," she enthused, "it was okay for me to be here. I was walking on tiptoe. Anything for the poet. Our relationship was like a spider web."[22]

The last image harks back to one in 'So Long, Marianne." Perhaps she felt she was in Marianne's shadow during these years. It annoyed her when Cohen's mother mistakenly called her by her name when they visited her in Canada. It was from force of habit.

Elrod went "country" in Franklin just as Cohen did, spending her time making dresses with a loom and writing poetry. At one stage she even attempted a pornographic novel to divert herself. Every so often she went back to Miami. Cohen became lonely in her absence. His song "Diamonds in the Mine," which he included on *Songs of Love and Hate,* berates her for not writing when she was away. There are "no letters in the mailbox."

Her absences eventually gave way to irritation. Other women filled the gap for him when she wasn't in Franklin.

Back in Montreal his infidelities continued. At one stage he was even rumoured to have seduced their 15-year-old *au pair.* Elrod had other men too, most notably Barrie Wexler. That betrayal cut deep with Cohen. Kelley Lynch once described Elrod as "a whore having sex with old men in coffins." [23]

As is the case with most of her remarks about Cohen, or anyone associated with him, one wouldn't be advised to take them seriously. Lynch enjoyed being sensationalistic. But she still knew what was going on. They spent a lot of time at loggerheads with one another, at times resembling the couple from Edward Albee's *Who's Afraid of Virginia Woolf?*

Cohen had many years of happiness with Marianne before the law of diminishing returns set in. With Elrod that happened much sooner. He knew from the outset that her personality was flintier, more obdurate. At times it even seemed as if he *wanted* a "cold and lonesome heroine." The dynamics of their relationship were totally different to the one he'd recently left. It was as if the tension of the music industry was personified by Elrod just as the relaxation of Hydra was by Marianne.

He feared her tempers and her bad moods. In many photographs taken of her from this time her expression seems either sullen or blank. She's rarely smiling. It's been said that "in all affiliations, the partner who loves least will always have the upper hand."[24] Elrod always had that – especially when she caught her man cheating on her.

When his career was going well, his love life never seemed to be. And vice versa. The touring which was once an ordeal for him now became a means of escape from an unendurable home situation. She suffered too. It was like a *folie a deux*.

In March 1972 he went to Nashville to prepare for a European tour. Before he began it he auditioned a few singers to back him,, among them Jennifer Warnes. She would go on to play a huge part in his life. "The reason I need girls to sing with me," he told her, "is that my voice depresses me."

Singing with Warnes, he thought, made him sound better. In future years the same applied to singing with Sharon Robinson and the Webb sisters, or Perla Batalla or Julie Christensen. The contrast between their falsettos and his base notes provided a contrasting richness of texture.

He played in the Royal Albert Hall in London in April. The atmosphere was electric. A reviewer of the show wrote, "Although the place was full to the brim, it was as if everybody sat next to an empty seat. You could have heard an unused tissue drop. It was a concentration that in many ways was awful with its intensity. It was a sin to cough.' [26] Such silences were a feature of many of his concerts in the years to come.

He returned to Montreal with Elrod in the summer, moving into a duplex with her on the Rue St. Dominique. She was pregnant.

He bought a row of apartments relatively cheaply in St. Dominique, remarking afterwards, "I should have gone into real estate. I'd have made a fortune".[27]

Some people believed Elrod became pregnant to hold on to him, that he was thinking of leaving her and this was her way of preventing that. They thought she lied to him about her "safe" period for having sex. The baby was born in September. They called him Adam. Cohen was in New York at the time, an indication of the fact that he wasn't much involved with the birth. There were rumours that Elrod had been sleeping with other men at the time she became pregnant, that the baby wasn't his.

The situation with her deteriorated further after Adam was born. Cohen was in London when the birth took place. He'd just received news of the death of his cousin Robert Hershorn from a heroin overdose in Hong Kong. He found it difficult to rejoice as much in being a father as he otherwise would have.

He was drinking and smoking a lot at this time. His doctor told him that if he didn't cut down on the cigarettes he could be dead within a year.

The warning stopped him in his tracks. He still carried a packet of cigarettes around with him afterwards but resisted opening it, referring to it as "a Parthenon in my pocket."[28]

He tried to keep his mind off his problems by writing. In 1973 he brought out another poetry book. *The Energy of Slaves* was illustrated by a poet called Daphne Richardson. She liked Cohen's work. At the time he collaborated with her she was a patient in a psychiatric hospital.

Her doctors thought she was delusional when she told them she was working with him. She wrote to him asking him to confirm that she was but he was touring at the time and didn't receive her letters. Richardson grew more and more frustrated and eventually became suicidal. When Cohen finally saw her letters and telegrams he asked his agent to confirm her story with a formal notification of their collaboration.

Tragically, it arrived too late. Three days before it got to her she jumped to her death from the headquarters of the BBC World Service in London, mentioning Cohen in a suicide note she wrote. It brought back the plight of his early guitar teacher to him.

Some of the most controversial lines he ever wrote appeared in the book. They concerned Norman Mailer. Cohen felt he'd recently been the victim of bullying by him. The lines go: "Dear Mailer, Don't ever fuck with me / Or I will kill you and your entire family." Mailer shivered when he read them, imploring Cohen not to publish the book in case it "inspired" some nutcase to do what he said. Cohen had been writing humorously of course but he understood Mailer's distress. He tried to stop the publication but it was too late.

He now recorded another album, *Live Songs*. Both the poetry book cover and the album sleeve featured him with a skinhead haircut.

This was a leaner, meaner Cohen. Gone was the clean-cut troubadour of the first three albums, at least for now. The hard typescript used for its title put the finishing touches to the image overhaul. With his thumb in his belt, a cigarette in his mouth and a "Fuck you" expression on his face, this definitely intimated songs more of hate than love.

War broke out between Israel and Egypt after the album came out. Cohen, to the surprise of many, decided to go to Tel Aviv and lend his support to Israel.

The war was also a way to get away from Elrod. "It's horrible between us," he railed, "I will go and stop Egypt's bullet." When he

79

got there he remarked, "The desert is beautiful. For a moment or two, you think your life is meaningful."[29]

Elrod suspended hostilities with him temporarily, putting a blue ribbon into his breast pocket before he left. It was intended as a kind of good luck charm. No matter how much they fought, she worried about his safety.

He was glad to be going to a place of significance, a place where people were fighting fire with fire. Surprisingly, considering his gentle nature, he didn't share the pacifistic ideals of the "Ban the Bomb" brigade. His attitude didn't jibe with the "Make love not war" code of the hippies but this hardly worried him. They'd already rejected him on various other counts like age and dress, if not religion. Why not give them another hook to hang him on? "One does not sit idly by the blood of one's brethren," he proclaimed, adding that pacifism "delights the hearts of killers."

The soldiers he sang to admired him for the way he ignored the creature comforts he was offered. He ate what they ate, drank what they drank, and slept rough.

He said he saw war as something wonderful, one of the few times in life when people were at their best because everyone was rooting for everyone else. A huge sense of community was created that one could never experience in any other situation.[30] Cohen was also fiercely proud of his father's military background.

One of the songs he sang at this time was "Lover, Lover, Lover (Come Back To Me)." It was an ambiguous track that was variously interpreted as either a call *to* a deity or *from* one. Was it anti-war? Cohen wouldn't say. "Many of my so-called anti-war songs," he suggested obliquely, "are also anti-peace."[31] His sex drive was as strong as ever when he was in Tel Aviv. During some of the interviews he did with female journalists while he was there he asked them to take off their clothes while they were interviewing him.

Elrod became pregnant again after he came back from Israel even though things were still bad between them. On his next album, *"New Skin for the Old Ceremony"* he sang, *"I live here with a woman and a child / The situation makes me nervous."* It was an understatement. He'd gone from one conflict to another, a military to a domestic one. "There is a war," he tells us, "a war between the man and the woman." Elsewhere he sings, "I tried to leave you/I don't deny/I closed the book on us/At least a hundred times." Sometimes when he was singing this song in concert he changed "a hundred times" to "a hundred thousand times."

The song titles read like an autopsy of the marriage, not only "There is a War" and "I Tried to Leave You" but also "Is This What You Wanted," "A Singer Must Die" and "Why Don't You Try." The latter song contains the line, "Do you need his labour for your baby?" This seems like a direct taunt to Elrod regarding his absence from Adam's birth. She gave him a hard time over that, thereby making sure he was present for the arrival of her next one.

The last song on the album, "Leaving Green Sleeves," is a reworking of a 16th century air but has the killer lines, "I reached for you but you were gone/So lady I'm going too." He could hardly have been more blunt about the fact that things were effectively over between them.

Another song on the album, "Chelsea Hotel #2," as mentioned, dealt with Janis Joplin, a very different kind of woman to Elrod but one who would probably have been equally difficult to live with.

It's uncharacteristically ungracious to Joplin, not only in the reference to her performing oral sex on him at the beginning but also in his reference to her as "ugly" (along with himself, to take the harm out of the word.) As a consolation they have "the music."

Cruelly, Joplin had been the victim of a fraternity campaign to have her voted the "ugliest man (sic) on campus" when she was a university student in Texas.[32] If we're to believe the words of the song, she preferred "handsome" men, but she was willing to "make an exception" for Cohen. Which was how they fell into the "unmade" bed together. Joplin apparently didn't enjoy their encounter, telling an interviewer afterwards that Cohen gave her nothing back after her exertions on his behalf.

He always beat himself up for the way he "kissed and told" about her. Some listeners felt he came across as debunking her for promiscuity.

Cohen himself thought he acted superior to her in the song. The reality of it was, "I'm still little Lenny, the 15-year-old Jewish kid from Montreal who couldn't get a date to save his life."[33]

Towards the end of the song he says he can't keep track of "each fallen robin." In the last line he says he doesn't think about her that often. Anyone who listens to it is entitled to say, "You could have fooled me," as a result of all the information he's given us about her up to now.

The liner notes said the song referred to "a singer who died a while ago." It wasn't until six years later, at a concert in Montreux, that he actually identified her as Joplin. It was a respectable time lapse but still went against his dictum, "I never discuss my mistresses or my tailors."[34]

Cohen didn't have a good time recording the album. He felt Columbia let him down with it. Not only did they interfere with his desired cover, which they deemed vulgar, but the sleeve notes described him as a "chronicler of despair." If his own company was colluding in cliched descriptions of him, what chance had he with the wider public of escaping such tags? He fought hard to have his cover retained and eventually Columbia relented.

He published a suicide note from Daphne Richardson on the sleeve. This was surely a precedent. Her mode of expression was Blakean.

She wrote, "I am inhabited by God and love bleeds and burns within me, but what caused the transfiguration was the mad mystic hammering of your body upon my body."

There was another tragedy that year. Jennifer Warnes' boyfriend was murdered. Cohen provided her with much comfort during this time. She'd been singing back-up for him since 1972. But along with death came life: he had another child by Elrod. This time it was a girl. He named her Lorca after the poet he loved so much.

Cohen recorded the album in New York rather than Nashville, and with John Lissauer rather than Bob Johnston.

He was happy with the way it turned out and he had every right to be. It was a welcome return to form for him in musical terms even if it was an evisceration of a relationship. Despite the fact that he was happy with the album, he found the tour gruelling.

Cohen told his backing group after a concert in New York: "I'm getting old. My nails are crumbling under the assault of the guitar strings. My throat is going. How many years more do I have of this? His comments suggested that stress over the situation with Elrod was getting to him. It wasn't like him to complain like that.

He even complained about the money he was earning. "I wanted to get paid for my work," he said obliquely, "but I didn't want to work for pay."[35] What was the difference? Maybe a sense of purity.

Elsewhere he's alleged to have said he started writing songs "to get laid, and later to get paid." This sounds very unCohenesque).

He often said that he was poorer after he became famous than before. In Hydra he'd lived on little over $1000 a year because of having such a basic existence.

With fame came expensive travel, hotel rooms, taxes, percentages to record producers, agents and so on. There was also a cost to his mental health as he left the "white rooms, and Marianne" for the concrete jungles of Montreal and New York.[36] Marianne went back to Norway after the relationship with Cohen ended but she still liked going to Greece from time to time.

Elrod went to Hydra in the summer of 1975. She was surprised to find Marianne in Cohen's house. She asked her to leave, which upset Marianne.

Cohen felt awkward. He'd had so many great times with her there before rejecting her. Now the rejection seemed to be doubled. Marianne was too much of a lady to argue with Elrod so she left. Cohen later offered to buy her a different house on the island but she wasn't interested.

Her heart was in number 764 – even though Elrod had revamped it to her tastes, injecting a lot of "Miami" into it.

Cohen's career, meanwhile, continued to prosper. Bob Dylan dedicated his 1975 album *Desire* to him, a huge honour. People had been saying they were rivals since Cohen started out but it wasn't the case. There was much mutual respect there.

Cohen once said he saw Dylan as his "brother." He saw them as working in the same area. "I feel he does it a little better than I do and sometimes I feel I do it a little better than he does but there's no competition between us. He has a worldwide audience. I have a tiny one."[37]

He often said he didn't want to be Dylan or any other kind of mega-star. Dylan was a planet; he was a satellite. He loved the "minor" poets, "the Robert Herricks and the guys who didn't talk about the huge concepts. They just spoke about their corners."[38]

Early on in his career Cohen was alleged to have said he wanted to be a Canadian Dylan. "I'd never say that," he protested, "any more than I'd say I wanted to be the next William Yeats."[39]

Both of them sang of "subterranean homesick blues," albeit with different emphases. Cohen knew Dylan's work was more spontaneous than his. Dylan, he said, had "hundreds of great lines that have the feeling of unhewn stone." His work was "inspired but not polished."[40] Maybe that was how he managed to do it so fast.

Cohen struggled with intransigent lines, finessing them like stones over weeks, months, even years. Dylan rode roughshod over them, adding other intransigent ones to them before coming (hopefully) to diamonds in the rough.

Cohen was more meticulous. In life he abided by the Zen dictate of "First thought, best thought" but in his work he felt songs didn't have to be written so much as re-written.

He worked slowly. That meant he wasn't as prolific as people like Dylan. So what? "I don't think mankind will be damaged," he told an interviewer in 1976, "if I don't put out a new album or a new book every year."

He was happy in his niche, a niche that was perhaps too easily identifiable for some people as he continued to re-cycle the songs that made him famous.

In a concert in Paris in 1976 he was asked to do twelve encores, six of them being for *'Suzanne."* He revelled in it. "Most singers have only one or two songs," he asserted, "if you're lucky you might have three."

Spector of Doom

Cohen spent the early part of 1976 working with John Lissauer on an album called *Songs for Rebecca*. It was subsequently abandoned. Marty Machat wanted him to collaborate with Phil Spector instead. Lissauer didn't know what was going on. Any calls he made to Cohen at this time went unanswered. Machat was impressed with the fact that Spector had recorded with members of The Beatles in the past, having produced John Lennon's *Imagine* and George Harrison's *All Things Must Pass*.

Machat didn't mind dumping Lissauer. He saw him as a discardable commodity. Neither Spector nor Cohen were doing well at this point. *New Skin For the Old Ceremony* hadn't sold well. A *Best of Leonard Cohen* album came out afterwards. These sorts of compilations always had overtones of desperation from production companies anxious to fill gaps. As for Spector, the market had changed since he was working with the Beatles. Glam rock had come in, and disco.

Spector was working for Warners. He owed the studio an album. Cohen was with Columbia (now CBS). Machat didn't think there'd be a problem in getting him released from that company as it was lukewarm about him. If he could get Cohen and Spector into a studio together, he thought, he could kill two birds with the one stone. The album would fulfil Spector's debt to Warners and hopefully give Cohen's career a shot in the arm.

It sounded good in theory. If Cohen did well with Spector it could spearhead his transition from the purist world where he was malingering to a more mainstream one that would attract the attention of younger listeners. On paper, however, Spector's theatrical

87

"Wall of Sound" style of production didn't look like a good fit for Cohen's more measured approach.

Machat regarded the idea as a poisoned chalice, seeing both Spector and Cohen as "commercial suicide." He took it on with an almost comic attitude, feeling that it was so weird it might just work.

The album was going to be called *Death of a Ladies Man*. Cohen would soon publish a book of poetry and prose called *Death of a Lady's Man*. Fans were invited to ponder on what the different spelling of the two titles was meant to signify – if they were bothered. Why was he engaging in such mischief? "I was trying to infect the public," he explained, "with the confusions I had at the time."[1]

Cohen appreciated Machat's point about him needing a career reboot. Despite his fear of going from the frying pan into the fire, the "weary boulevardier" was still looking forward to the adventure.[2]

Spector's motivation for the collaboration was less clear. "I like Leonard," he insisted. He wanted to work with him even if the record they produced was going to, as he put it, "sell shit."[3]

Cohen felt he had certain things in common with Spector; not only his Jewishness but the fact that both of them had lost their fathers at a young age. Spector's one had committed suicide.

Spector lived in a mansion that once belonged to Bela Lugosi, the famous Dracula star. Cohen saw the danger of being in the presence of such a volatile man after he was invited to dinner with him one night with Elrod. When they got up to leave he ordered them to sit down again, even going so far as to lock the doors to keep them there. He'd recently been thrown through the windshield of his car and suffered multiple injuries from it. The accident caused an erratic man to become even more erratic.

He spent most of the dinner abusing his staff. Always the kind of person to make the best of a bad situation, Cohen said to him at one stage, "To salvage the evening, rather than watch you shout at your servants, let's do something more interesting."[4] Spector was agreeable to Cohen's suggestion so they sat down at his piano together. They stayed up all night working on an arrangement of Patti Page's "I Went to Your Wedding."

On their first night in the recording studio they also stayed up all night. Cohen was worked to the bone. He only got breaks when Spector went to the rest room. It was difficult to perform in such an environment. Spector's assistant Devra Robitaille recalled, "It was Dickensian. Very drab and gloomy. Big velvet curtains, always kept shut. Never any sunlight. I kept expecting to find Miss Havisham in one of the rooms, wearing her wedding dress and covered in cobwebs."[5] Robitaille had been Spector's lover in the past. She would later work with Cohen, telling people he was so nice he "ruined" her chances of working for anyone else.

Spector was loud and bombastic. His military flourishes contrasted markedly with the recondite intimacies one associated with Cohen. He was the ringmaster, grinding everyone into submission as he cracked his whip. Cohen gazed transfixed at the vaudevillian spectacle.

There were 27 musicians, 15 back-up singers and 4 sound engineers. In the middle of it all were Cohen and Spector, the tyrant and his victim, both searching for uplifts in their declining careers.

Drink was served, but not food. That would have been too prosaic. Cohen eventually started to imbibe. It was a case of, "If you can't beat 'em, join 'em."

Spector usually had a bottle of wine in one hand and a pistol in the other. At one point he famously cocked the pistol and put it to Cohen's head saying, "I love you, Leonard." Cohen replied, "I hope you do, Phil."[6] "I expected him to be eccentric," Cohen said, "What I didn't know was that he was mad."

Bob Dylan stumbled into the studio on the second night. He was breaking up from his wife Sarah at the time and had a woman on each shoulder. He was slugging whiskey. Allen Ginsberg came in behind him with his lover, the poet Peter Orlovsky. Ginsberg was staying with Dylan at this time while Dylan edited his film *Renaldo and Clara*. Spector joked that there were so many Jews in the room they could have had a bar mitzvah.

It wasn't long before he co-opted Dylan to join in the song they were cutting at the time, "Don't Go Home With Your Hard-On." It didn't sound like something either Dylan or Cohen would usually put their voices to but the atmosphere led to them throwing themselves into it full tilt. Spector never had it so good. It was the kind of anarchy he thrived on. In the course of the song Dylan slid down his microphone and started singing from the floor. Nobody batted an eyelid.[7]

It's doubtful if Dylan would have succumbed to such a pantomime if the roles were reversed and Spector had stumbled into his own recording studio in this manner during a production. The Irish author Eamonn Sweeney reflected, "Bob probably thought with some glee, 'Well, there's another rival's career fucked.'" It isn't the worst song on the album but that's not saying much.

One got the sense of Spector rubbing Cohen's face in his poor sales by reducing him to the lowest common denominator of public taste. The fact that Cohen was willing to go along with it seemed like a capitulation to Spector's mindset. The song sounded more like a Rolling Stones number than anything else. In this and in some of the other tracks on the album it was as if Spector was trying to muffle Cohen's voice under a plethora of sound effects. He should have known better. A Cohen album that didn't highlight his voice was always going to be its own worst enemy.

His voice sounds tame on it. It's as if he's singing from behind a wall, or under water. There was no "tower of song" here, just a mausoleum of noise. It was like trying to sing when someone was drilling the street outside. One night Spector turned everything up so loud he blew one of the speakers. Another night he screamed, "Anyone laidback in the room, get the fuck out of here!"[8]

He treated Cohen like another member of his crew, nothing more. As one writer remarked, he was like a "walk-on actor in his own movie."[9] Except of course it wasn't his movie. It was Spector's. He decided to let him have his way. There didn't seem to be any alternative.

Spector's bodyguards roamed around the studio in various stages of intoxication. There were guns everywhere. "You were slipping over bullets," Cohen railed, "You were biting into revolvers in your hamburger."

At one point, probably with too much wine in him, he challenged one of the bodyguards to draw on him, calling him a "fucking pussycat" who probably didn't even know "how to use that thing."[10] The bodyguard declined the challenge, which was probably for the best. For both of them.

He thought of throwing in the towel more than once but didn't. Maybe, like Machat, he felt it was so crazy a collaboration a marriage made in hell – it might just work. There was also a sense in which Cohen felt just as "flipped out" as Spector was – mainly thanks to the wine.

On a one-to-one level he liked Spector. The problem with him was when he became carried away with an audience, when he turned into "a performer with a kind of Medici magnitude."[11]

He had an "Anything goes" attitude to the album. One night a drummer, Jim Keltner, fell off his stool and clattered to the floor. Spector kept the sound in as an extra drumbeat.

Another evening he pulled a gun on his violin player, Bobby Bruce. Bruce walked out.

The title song took hours to record. It started at 7.30 one evening but by 2.30 am little progress had been made. The musicians had been on double time since midnight. After 2 am that became quadruple time. It was 4 a.m. before Spector was ready for Cohen to start singing.[12]

"It was all about control," he said, "The music was subsidiary." Spector had his guards take the tapes away every night – or morning – to be put under lock and key.

The flipside of that control was Spector's Pythonesque sense. One night he turned up in a surgeon's outfit carrying a baton. Shortly afterwards he did one of his disappearing acts into the bathroom, probably to ingest something.

"Mixing booze with the kind of exaggerated ego that comes with a high school nerd made good," as one writer put it, Spector was "as much a performer in his living room as most rock stars were on stage." By now Cohen was beyond being shocked. When you were in the last ditch, as Beckett once said, all you could do was sing.

It might have proved to be an enjoyable spectacle if one wasn't freezing to death. That was another problem.

The temperature was 30 degrees outside but Spector had the air conditioning turned down to almost freezing point. It furthered the sense of absurdity Cohen was feeling. Some nights he found himself wearing a fur coat to stave off hypothermia.

Spector didn't care who lived or died. He was too immersed in his production: "A play by Phil Spector produced by Phil Spector starring Phil Sepctor."[13]

Cohen never got a chance to finish his contribution to the album. Spector "decided" when it was complete. He didn't give Cohen a chance to re-cut the final track despite repeated requests to do so. He was outraged, but by now he'd become tired of it all. He decided to do nothing, to let the chips fall where they would.

"I'd have had to hire a private army to get the tapes from him," he reasoned, "I kept my sanity by walking away."

Cohen didn't leave Spector so much as escape from him. Arguing with him over the final cut, he surmised, could have led to another "imprisonment" in his mansion, or another pistol jammed in his ear. Keeping schtum was damage limitation.

He disowned the album, even going so far as to pay $20,000 to release himself from its promotion. It was seen as a career-killer for him by the media. Rolling Stone referred to it as his "doo-wap nightmare."[14] He himself dismissed it as "masturbatory junk." Basically he felt he was wrong for Spector from the outset. "Tina Turner should have made the album with Bill Medley," he suggested.[15]

Cohen wasn't the only person who disowned the album. So did Spector and Warners. Machat had to almost beg Warners to release it, arguing that the combination of Spector and Cohen would give it sales potential no matter how bad it was. They reluctantly agreed to do so on that rather tenuous basis. This, after all, was the premise upon which the deal was brokered. So it came out – against the odds. The cover showed Cohen sitting serenely between Elrod (looking familiarly sullen) and a Quebec model called Eva La Pierre that he'd met in Hydra.

"There are four seconds on it," he said, "that are music." But he never regretted making it. It was an interesting experiment for him. Today it has a kind of cult appeal. Curiosity surrounds some of its lesser-known tracks: "Fingerprints," "Iodine," "Memories," "True Love Leaves No Traces."

The lyrics of many of the songs stand up as well as those from any of his albums, especially those adapted from his poetry, which makes Spector's skewered "packaging" of them particularly reprehensible. If one could airbrush his arrangements out of them we might have a purer album.

Maybe some future technology could bring this about. In the meantime, one has to be content with the numbers which somehow seem to have escaped his interference, like the superb 'I Left a Woman Waiting," and the climactic title track, recorded under duress but still packing a punch.

Cohen said of Spector afterwards that he didn't think he could tolerate "any other shadows in his darkness." The album sold less than any other one in his whole career. Spector blamed Cohen for this, saying snidely to a friend that he got hate mail "from all eight of Leonard's fans." He went on to align him to, of all things, the Partridge family.[16]

Cohen dined out on stories of working with Spector. Asked if the sessions were as crazy as people said, he'd reply, "Crazier".[17] But time mellowed him. He grew to have a strange fascination for the album, even an affection for it, "like a parent for a handicapped child."

He saw it as his most autobiographical album from the point of view that it contained both his spiritual and earthy sides. "Everybody," he chuckled, "will now know that within this serene Buddhist interior there beats an adolescent heart."[18]

Crawling From the Wreckage

Cohen's Buddhist side was more in evidence the following year when Leo Sayer released a song called "When I Need You." It bore a strong resemblance to "Famous Blue Raincoat" in one of its sequences.

The part of the song under scrutiny was from the phrase "Jane came by" to "planned to go clear," a total of seventeen notes. Fourteen was the threshold for plagiarism. Machat sued Sayer's record label for a huge amount.

Cohen said he wasn't interested in the action. They settled out of court for a much smaller amount, a mere 15% of the royalties. The concession was an admission of liability. Machat was furious with Cohen. His reluctance to go to court had weakened his bargaining position immeasurably. "They smelt insecurity on our part," he said. Of course it wasn't that.

He wasn't litigious. That had been obvious when he put up with Jeff Chase stabbing him in the back at the beginning of his career, telling people that "Suzanne" was "too pure" a song to make money from. Did he feel the same about "Famous Blue Raincoat"? "I probably got the melody from somewhere else myself," he told Machat. It was the last thing the money-hungry executive wanted to hear.

Cohen had more pressing problems than money now. His relationship with Elrod was in worse trouble than ever. She couldn't cope with his mood swings. He was like two people, she complained, loving her when he was with her but not with her – or the children – enough.

Both Cohen and Elrod had progressive ideas of parenting. In some ways they were like hippies. The children were left to their own devices a lot of the time. Sometimes they were found wandering the streets late at night. Adam once said he grew up in "a circus with two tents."

Elrod was also becoming increasingly angered by Cohen's growing list of lovers, many of which he didn't bother even hiding anymore. Kim Harwood was one of these in the late seventies.

There was never a question they'd marry or even live together and she accepted that. He called her whenever he felt like it. When she was with him he was always attentive to her but then one day he stopped calling her. She accepted that too. It was the deal with him. Things went on for a while and then they stopped without explanation.

Elrod wasn't as easy-going as Harwood. Whenever he mistreated her, or she believed he'd done so, she let him know all about it. She once showed him a painting of a ladybug crawling into a bouquet of flowers.

"You're the bug," she snorted as she presented it to him. Such gestures weren't infrequent during their marriage. She felt he projected a different image towards the public. In that he would have been the flower – and perhaps she would have been the bug.

His mother developed leukaemia in 1978. Elrod was in Miami at the time. He phoned her to give her the news. She flew to Montreal to say her goodbyes to her, becoming as close as she could to Cohen during these days. Masha died in March of that year.

He was sad to lose her. She was a force of nature, larger than life in many ways. The fact that she was without Nathan for so long drew her closer to him, sometimes closer than he would have wished. As with all the other women in his life, he tried to keep in charge of how big a part she played in it.

With Elrod that wasn't always possible. It became less possible than ever now. No sooner was Masha in the grave than they started arguing again.

She left him in April, taking off for France with the children to make a new life for the three of them in a farm she bought outside Marseilles.

Within a month Cohen had lost the two women at the centre of his life. He took tablets like Prozac and Desyrel to deal with his depression. Where was his gypsy wife tonight?

Despite the bitterness of the split with Elrod, or maybe because of it, he tried his best to have a healthy relationship with Adam and Lorca, spending as much time with them as he could in his busy schedule. They spent all their holidays with him, going to Hydra in the summers and Montreal in the winters.

Elrod kept a tight rein on them for the rest of the time. She accused him of not being interested in them, of being more focused on his music. He in turn accused her of keeping them from him. The arguments between them went round in circles.

In the past, such arguments tended to be about things like their various bed partners. Now they were mainly about money and travel arrangements.

Cohen had legal custody of them. In this capacity he was consulted about matters like their schooling and medical care. Unfortunately, he didn't get to spend much "quality time" with them, as the expression went, outside holiday periods.

It was time-consuming for him travelling from Los Angeles to see them. He had to fly from L.A. to New York and fly from there to

Paris. He then took a tram to Marseilles and a bus or cab to the farm. The first time he visited them, Elrod wouldn't let him into the house. He had to talk to them from the cab.

He later bought a trailer near the farm. It made things a little easier but her bitterness with him never went away. Some people would say such bitterness was justified. She'd been betrayed by him so much.

He asked her questions about them but she kept tight-lipped. Had he travelled all these miles for this? What was the point? Would it come to a stage where his children didn't know him? That they saw him – like her – as a singer and a writer instead of a person?

He knew so little about their "missing years." Had she told them not to open up to him? To grudge them information about themselves as she was doing?

She rationed both time and information to him regarding them, ladling it out like something he didn't deserve. "You expect our lives to stop when you get here," she accused once.

He said it wasn't like that, that he wanted things to go on as they always did, with him as a part of them.

She told him he was in love with fame, with his ego. It was like revenge for the fact that things hadn't worked out between them. She was "la belle dame sans merci."

He thought back to how it was when they first met, the magic of those early months, the excitement, the infatuation, her dark good looks and her mystery. All that had been gone for a long time now, replaced by wars of words between them as his children grew up without him.

Would things have been less bad if he hadn't had them? He wouldn't have needed her to be in his life then. They wouldn't be

99

hurling abuse at one another. Children became weapons when couples split up. In such cases the women usually held all the aces.

He sometimes told people he never wanted children. Maybe he was as poor a father as he was a lover. Was he the problem or was it her?

Things had been so different with Marianne. She gave him everything of herself, and everything of Axel, a child he hadn't even brought into the world. He was presented with him lovingly to spend as much time with him as he wanted.

Marianne loved seeing Axel enjoying him, watching the way his eyes lit up when he came into a room, when he played his guitar, when he scratched words on a page. He saw that with Adam and Lorca sometimes too but Elrod didn't want it. She scowled when he was getting on with them. Was she afraid he'd take them away from her one day? That they might even grow to love him more than her in time?

"You're only here when it suits you," she rasped. It was just one in a series of cynical comments about him. How could he explain to her that he tried to save up every available moment he had to be in this tiny trailer, doing his best to make it seem like a home when it wasn't much more than a glorified hotel room? There were times he felt that if he stood on his head it wouldn't have been enough for her. Too many wounds had festered.

"You can go now, Mr Singer Man," she'd say at the end of his visits, making out that it was a relief to him when the reality was that his heart was breaking.

"Will you write a poem about being here?" she'd taunt, "or another song? "So Long, Marianne," perhaps?" He understood now what people meant when they said they were prisoners of their fame. It was a poisoned chalice.

His relationship with Elrod began at the start of the seventies and ended at the end of the decade just as his one with Marianne began at the start of the sixties and ended at the end of that decade. The pattern of euphoria descended into frustration before segueing into a long goodbye in both of the time frames.

Was this as long as he could spend with a woman? Had his love life a built-in obsolescence to it? Who would his woman of the eighties be, people wondered. Would she too occupy the "loser's corner" as the decade progressed?

Marianne married a man called Jan Stang in 1979. He had three daughters from an earlier marriage and she became a stepmother to them. It was like a reversal of her situation with Cohen after he'd become a surrogate father to young Axel.

She visited Hydra with Stang that summer. They were walking along a coastal path one day when they ran into Cohen. He was with his friend Virginia Yelletisch.

Marianne stumbled as Cohen introduced Yelletisch to her. He didn't try to stop her falling. Instead he looked at Yelletisch to help, which she did.

It was an interesting incident. Yelletisch thought Marianne looked at Cohen expectantly. It was as if she thought there was still something between them. By not moving to help her he was letting her know there wasn't. It's surprising that she didn't reach out to Stang instead of to her old lover.

Cohen's next album was called *Recent Songs*. It was, he joked, the most perfect title he'd ever been able to come up with. This was a misnomer as three of the songs went back to 1975. It was recorded in L.A. and produced by himself and Henry Lewy.

It was his first album not to chart, despite having many elegiac tracks on it like "The Traitor" and "The Window." "Came So Far For Beauty," which featured John Lissauer (who co-wrote it with him) on piano, is also heart-rending. Jennifer Warnes and Sharon Robinson both sing on "The Guests" in what proved to be a foretaste of much more to come from them with him.

Cohen showed a softer tone to Elrod than he did in *New Skin For the Old Ceremony* in songs like "Humbled in Love" and "The Smokey Life." This was the original title of the album.

He's also gentle in the majestic "The Gypsy's Wife." It's as if time has healed the hurt of their parting. The album was a slow burner. It's grown in stature with time.

As he prepared to embark on a tour with it, Warnes asked if she could accompany him. He didn't think this was a good idea, fearing it might get in the way of her solo career, but she wanted it so much he agreed. Little did either of them know then how immersed they would soon be in one another's lives.

Bob Dylan converted to Christianity that year, bringing out a trilogy of "born again" albums: *Slow Train Coming*, *"Saved"* and *Shot of Love*. Some of his fans deserted him at this time, feeling the (in)famous iconoclast had betrayed them by getting, as it were, God on his side.

Many of his Jewish fans felt particularly aggrieved. Cohen was confused. "I don't get the Jesus part," he sniffed.[1] But he thought the songs were brilliant. They were "some of the most beautiful songs that ever entered the landscape of popular music."[2]

His economic circumstances improved as the new decade began. He received revenue from concerts as well as books and some cover versions of his songs that had been recorded. His payments to Elrod also lessened as Adam and Lorca grew up.

He did more concerts than usual in 1980. They were sell-outs and he often received standing ovations. At one of them he thanked the audience for "your interest in my work, for letting me live the life of the heart, and for not believing the shit they write about me."

He was referring to the number of critics who still pigeonholed him as the lugubrious baritone who was out of touch with modern music. U2's Bono quipped, "It was against the law to listen to Leonard in the days of punk."[3]

He seemed like an anachronism to many people during the eighties. It was the age of "skinny ties, button-down collars, drainpipe trousers, pork pie hats, Chelsea boots and parkas."

The Who were in, The Kinks were in, Quadrophenia were in, "and everybody's Daddy was buying them a Lambretta for their 18th birthday."[4] In such a world, his soulful yearnings took listeners on odysseys to places they didn't necessarily want to go.

Cohen spent the early years of the eighties gravitating between Hydra, France, Manhattan and Montreal. He continued to argue with Elrod when he was in France but not as much, she insisted, as the newspapers would have people believe.

One source of argumentation between them was her unwillingness to bring the children up in the Jewish faith. She said there were no synagogues near her in France but Cohen didn't notice her being inclined to seek them out in Montreal either when she was there.

103

His romances went on as before. They were more carefree now that they didn't involve any subterfuge with Elrod. He was a magnet for women with his courteous ways and old world charm, but he still adopted a "Love 'em and leave 'em" attitude when it came to mating rituals.

He told Felicity Buriski, a British actress he'd been seeing every so often over the years, "You're the only woman I've ever considered marrying." Barrie Wexler deadpanned, "He should have added, 'This month.'"[5]

He never ceased to be surprised when women threw themselves at him. He thought they'd have been more likely to do this if he was an alpha male. Usually it worked the other way. Ever since the Judy Collins meltdown he should have remembered that it was his "little boy lost" aura that was his trump card in this department. He stopped to conquer.

Some people told him being a poet was like an aphrodisiac to a woman. He didn't find that to be so. Fans from afar might have wanted to make love to him after reading his works – he received letters to that effect – but when it came down to it, success with women became largely aligned with chemistry, with who was attracted to him physically, with the heat of the moment.

That wasn't to say the beauty of his lyrics didn't help, but they weren't the whole thing. "Women are a dangerous arena," he said, "as the heart is always opening and closing. Eventually the accumulation of defeats gets to you. You have no life jacket."[6]

Cohen once had a discussion with Barrie Wexler about the best way to seduce a woman. He thought washing the dishes was a good idea. Wexler believed doing her laundry was a better one.

Cohen said, "If you don't do the dishes you might never get to the laundry!" At times like this he showed that "adolescent heart" he sometimes talked about.

Behind all the conquests he was still the young man who patrolled Montreal in Mort Rosengarten's car, still the lost soul "walking the streets of New York at three in the morning, trying to strike up conversations with the women selling cigarettes in hotels."[7]

He never went along with the image of himself as a ladies man. "For someone who's spent 2500 nights alone," he contended, "It's a ridiculous description." He wasn't even "in the ball game." (And he had a thousand women to prove it).

He dated the Costa Rican artist/model Gabriela Valenzuela on and off from 1982 to 1986. They had a passionate relationship but once again he failed to commit himself exclusively to her – or to discuss the dreaded "M" word with her.

A Zen friend, Marcia Raden, asked him once why he never married. "Because I'm not good at it," he said simply, "Why should I do that to somebody?" It's curious that he said "I'm not good at it" instead of "I wouldn't be good at it."

Aviva Layton perhaps put her finger on the problem when she said, "Poets don't generally make good husbands."[8]

Cohen said he never took women serious enough to marry them. Maybe it would be truer to say he took them too seriously to do so. Knowing he wouldn't be able to tie himself to one indefinitely, it didn't make sense to commit to that kind of bond, or bondage. "Being a monk is easy," he believed, "Dealing with one-on-one relationships is tough."[9]

One of the reasons being a monk was easy for him was because it didn't involve a vow of celibacy. A phrase he used often in his life was "the voluptuousness of austerity."[10]

He didn't see a dichotomy between the sacred and the sensual. "If God is left out of sex," he argued, "it becomes pornographic. If sex is left out of God, it becomes self-righteous."[11]

Back in the Game

The early eighties aren't generally regarded as seminal years in Cohen's life but he kept himself busy during this time. In some ways it could be argued that it paved the way for the renaissance he experienced towards the end of the decade. Even in the lean years he still had a loyal band of devotees rooting for him. Cohen's friend Alan Twigg quit his job at CBC Radio in the early 1980s when his boss told him he found Cohen boring.

In 1983 in Hydra he met a French fashion photographer called Dominique Issermann. She became an important figure in his life, directing two of his videos ("Dance Me to the End of Love" and "First We Take Manhattan") as well as living with him. She was one of many lovers he had whose names ended with the same sound, like Suzanne, Marianne and Sherman.

In 1984 he made a 30-minute video called "I Am a Hotel." This is a curious little film. It has a kind of smoky elegance about it, and a Big Band sound reminiscent of Phil Spector at his best. It was shot in the King Edward Hotel in Toronto but looks more like France. Filmed entirely without dialogue, all we're missing is the appearance of Marcel Marceau in clown make-up as the semi-surreal scenarios unfold. Barrie Wexler produced it.

It was made at a time when videos seemed *de rigueur* for singers. The difference here is that it's thirty minutes in length rather than five, and has a more extensive "plot" than the average video. Thus we see various dalliances playing themselves out in balletic form - a chambermaid and a bellboy engaging in all sorts of contortions, a *femme fatale* courting her beau...and Cohen ("The Resident")

107

removed from it all like some urbane sophisticate as he nonchalantly smokes cigarettes and blows rings into the air.

He didn't want to make it, becoming even more reluctant when the funding dried up. Wexler somehow saved the project from perishing due to some frantic late night phone calls to the Canada Film Development Corporation as he tried desperately to hide the problems from his leading star.

The songs are brilliantly executed. "The Guests" bookends the other numbers ("Memories," "The Gypsy's Wife," "Chelsea Hotel #2" and "Suzanne" in the film's stylised envelope pattern. Shot in just six days, it cost $250,000. This appears exorbitant for such a short running time but the money is all up there on the screen. In time Cohen came to admire it, despite his initial misgivings. It won a Golden Rose Award at the 24th International Montreux Festival in 1984, seeing off 32 other entrants in a surprise victory.

At this time, Cohen also worked on a libretto called *Night Magic* which he made with his Canadian friend Lewis Furey. It was a curious piece which he described as being "a combination of Brecht and Disney." [1]

The following year Jeff Chase offered to return the rights to his three "stolen" songs to him - at least if the price was right. When Chase asked him how much he was going to give him for them, an outraged Cohen was alleged to have replied, in one of the few instances we have of him using expletives outside his books, " One dollar, you motherfucker."[2]

His attitude was understandable but sounded decidedly different from the man who said he believed "Suzanne" was too pure a song to make money from. Clearly, all the years of having his signature tune taken out of his control had weighed heavily on him.

Cohen now reunited with John Lissauer to record *Various Positions*. He hadn't worked with him since the abandoned *Songs for Rebecca* in the mid-seventies.

He employed Leanne Ungar as his sound engineer for the album. It was the beginning of a very fruitful partnership. "If you're going to spend time locked in a small room with someone," she said, "you'd better get along with them." That was easy with Cohen - especially if you were a woman.

The album had one of his favourite songs on it, "If It Be Your Will." Is this a song or a poem? Maybe it's a prayer. Cohen always sang it with great feeling, leaving one in little doubt how much he thought of it.

Other stand-outs from a much-neglected milestone in Cohen's canon are 'Night Comes On" (a kind of precursor to Dylan's "Not Dark Yet") "Dance Me to the End of Love," which he sang to open his shows in later years - with Jennifer Warnes again providing backing vocals – and "Coming Back to You," a song that seems to suggest the Elrod phase of his life is being revisited.

It also had "Hallelujah." I use the word "also" deliberately. The point is that nobody really noticed it at the time. It was seen as another ordinary track on an ordinary album. Walter Yetnikoff was still at the helm in CBS at this time. He'd never liked Cohen, even after his career went into the stratosphere.

Cohen kept adding verses to 'Hallelujah." At one point he found himself on the floor of a hotel in his underwear, banging his head on the floor and saying to himself, "I can't finish this song."[3]

109

It lurked in the undergrowth for years after its appearance on Side Two of this album, Bob Dylan being one of the few people to give it credit (and sing it in his concerts) at the time of its release.

Columbia didn't release *Various Positions* in the U.S. Cohen wasn't too upset by this. He saw his main fanbase as being elsewhere. "Walter Yetnikoff wanted me to be Dylan," he groaned, "He never forgave me for not being him."

One of the problems for Yetnikoff was the funereal overtones of the aforementioned "Dance Me to the End of Love" and "Night Comes On." Such songs didn't seem marketable to him. Despite their heart-scorching beauty they seemed to have intimations of mortality about them. Had Cohen the "end of the road" in his sights?

Elrod moved back to New York in the early eighties. She bought a brownstone there. The change of quarters didn't improve her attitude to Cohen. Eric Lerner visited him one day in 1984 when he was there with Adam and Lorca. Elrod was out when he arrived. When she came home she hardly acknowledged either of them. Her dress was black and so was her mood

Cohen took the children to a tacky restaurant to eat. While he was there he told Lerner about his life with her. He said she could treat him any way she liked because of the absence of "no fault" divorces in New York. It meant she could portray him as the bad guy indefinitely. (Cohen often spoke of his relationship to Elrod like a marriage, and their parting like a divorce).

He was fifty now. He didn't have a problem with that. "Policemen call me 'Sir,'" he trilled, "Old ladies give me their seats on buses." He said he saw himself like a Volvo car. Volvos were reputed to last 23 years. That was how long he'd been in the music business. "I have no regrets if it stops now," he declared, "I'm grateful for all the things I've got."

"Grateful" was a word he used often. Because he'd come to music through the side door of literature, he felt everything that came his way afterwards was a bonus. After years of being bashful reading his poems to audiences, he'd reinvented himself as a performer. The longer that continued, the more comfortable he became with it. Gone were the years when he was nervous before people.

He once invited an entire audience to get up on the stage with him. Another night he invited them back to his room. The warmth of these gestures was typical of him. In a business dominated by "young men in a hurry," Cohen's geniality became one of his most attractive features.

His willingness to extend the hand of friendship reached absurd levels on occasion. On a German tour once, a man said he wanted to shoot him. Instead of calling the police, he brought him up on stage with him so he could watch the concert.

In March 1985 he played a show in Dublin that also demonstrated his caring nature. A cousin of the musician Glen Hansard suffered a seizure during the show. Cohen insisted on seeing him after it to make sure he was all right. As he greeted him, Hansard said he'd never forget his "soft, firm"" handshake. That was the moment, Hansard vowed, that he would become a musician and carry on such humanity. He "floated" home singing Cohen's songs.

He appeared at the Kalvoya Festival in Norway that June, looking very trendy in an uncharacteristic yellow jacket. He had his hair slicked back and was unshaven. It was an outdoor event, like a Norwegian Woodstock in a way, with many of the men in the audience looking like hippies in their bare chests as they joked with their women and children. Cohen got into the spirit of it immediately, barking out a brilliant rendition of "Memories."

When he introduced his band members they slow-handclapped him amusedly. Anjani Thomas was giggling at the side of the stage. "This is my Honolulu friend," he announced to the gathering, "my pearl of the Pacific. She has a mean streak and that's what I love most about her. It brings out her passionate fire."

The following year he wrote "Take This Waltz," a song he adapted from a Lorca poem to mark the fiftieth anniversary of his death. He worked painstakingly to get it right. It took him 150 hours to finish it.

He did a "blink and you miss him" cameo role in the TV series *Miami Vice* in 1986. It wasn't his choice. His children made him do it. It was one of the "must see" programmes of the time for young people.

He played an executive in the French Secret Service who was trying to blow up some Greenpeace boats. His part was originally substantial but was cut down to just a minute in the end. He knew it was time to get worried when the people producing the programme kept telling him he was great.

Their praise was so excessive he suspected there was something behind it that they weren't telling him. "Does that mean I'm useless?" he asked them. They replied, "We're afraid so."

He didn't tell Adam and Lorca he was going to be in it at all. They were watching the programme one night when he appeared on it out of the blue. "Their excitement," he said, "made up for the fact that I knew I could never be an actor." The year was most notable for the fact that he managed to get the rights back to the three songs Jeff Chase had taken from all those years ago when Cohen walked away from the demo tape Chase was recording with him. The fee was $75,000, an astronomical price for something that should never have been an issue in the first place.

He was alleged to have said to Chase prior to the deal, "Give me those songs back or I'll fucking kill you." He got them back all right, but for a little more than the dollar he'd offered him a few years before.

Between 1986 and 1987 he commuted between Marseilles and Paris. He'd spend some time with Adam and Lorca and then fly back to Paris to see Dominique Issermann. Afterwards it was back to L.A. or Montreal, or both.

He was living a life of "planes, trains and automobiles" as he tried to juggle the various elements of his life.

Jennifer Warnes recorded a landmark album of his songs in 1987 called *Famous Blue Raincoat*. It had been on her mind to do it for years. She'd sung for and with him in so many of his concerts and albums, perhaps it was an inevitable progression from those.

As well as being a collaborator of his, she was also a close friend - and his conduit to a wider public. "I'm the waitress," she said, "I'm bringing the food." She described the album as being like walking around in an attic, shining a flashlight on unrecognized gems." It said to people, "Have you forgotten what's beautiful?"

It cast a wide net, containing material all the way from *Songs From a Room* to *Various Positions*. Warnes did more than justice to it. In all the years since, one would be hard pressed to find more haunting covers of his songs than here, especially "Joan of Arc" and "Song of Bernadette."

Warnes wrote the latter song. Cohen helped her with some of the lines. She was a Catholic with a devotion to St Bernadette. She was originally named Bernadette but her siblings preferred Jennifer so the name was changed a week after her birth. She'd been inspired to write it while sitting in a bus close to Lourdes.

Other numbers included "Came So Far for Beauty" which, as mentioned, Cohen co-wrote with John Lissauer, and two tracks from the not-yet-released *I'm Your Man* album, "First We Take Manhattan" and "Ain't No Cure For Love."

Warnes sang her heart out. It went down a storm with the public, resulting in Cohen's name being on everyone's lips again after some years in relative obscurity. Needless to say, it increased her own profile as well. She'd been relatively quiet since winning a Best Original Song Oscar for "Up Where We Belong," which she recorded with Joe Cocker in 1983 for the film *An Officer and a Gentleman*. It was written by Buffy Sainte-Marie. Sainte-Marie had been following Cohen's career with some interest since they first hooked up in New York in the mid-sixties.

He never minded if people had better success with his songs than he did. He was merely flattered that they sang them, be they Judy Collins with "Suzanne" or Warnes with this album. He never criticised a cover version of one of his songs, feeling that it was the ultimate honour to an artist that someone chose to adapt his material. "My critical faculties," he said, "go into suspended animation when someone covers one of my songs."[4] If they became famous in the process, good luck to them.

It worked the other way too. Singers who had iconic songs like say Procul Harum with "A Whiter Shade of Pale" or Peter Sarstedt with "Where Do You Go To My Lovely" sometimes became identified with them to the exclusion of anything else they did. In some cases that might not have been much. Cohen often said he worked in a small corner. "I'm a satellite," he liked to say, "rather than a planet." He was being typically self-deprecating here. It was a very big corner. But one took his point.

He didn't like the image of himself as a guru. More preferable to him was the idea of writing songs to listen to while he was washing the dishes: "Something to set the mood while you're reaching for a lady's hand. Something to fill the air when its too empty." He wanted to write "the sort of songs you hear on the car radio." Sometimes he did, but not too often. Warnes turned them into that with her alchemy.

Cohen always felt she was under-rated. "She has the best pipes in the business," he praised. He compared her voice to the Californian weather, saying, "It seems very sunny but there's an earthquake behind it."

He originally wanted to call the album *Jenny Sings Lenny* but CBS thought that sounded too trite. In the liner notes, however, he was allowed feature a cartoon with him handing her a torch with those three words on it.

Warnes made his songs more popular than they were when sung by himself just as Judy Collins had years before. His fanbase was largely female so this made sense. The secret was to change the gender – or even identity – of the singer in the song without making it too noticeable. This was tricky with the title song, which ends with the words *"Sincerely, L. Cohen"* but Warnes' voice was so powerful she got away with it.

Warnes had a brief fling with Cohen. She was one in a long line of women he was seeing at this time. That didn't work for her so she drew away from him. Like Suzanne Verdal, she felt physical contact could jeopardise their friendship.

Cohen's next album, *I'm Your Man,* came out shortly after *Famous Blue Raincoat.* It was his first self-produced one. Almost every song on it is a classic. This was the first time people heard the voice of Sharon Robinson in any significant degree. He'd worked with her on his 1979 release *Field Commander Cohen* but she only sang back-up on that.

The album gives us all sorts of mixed signals. One writer surmised, "It's the most fun you can have while being told that life is a terrible joke." Age is catching up on him, he tells us in "Tower of Song." He aches in the places where he used to play. But you get the feeling he's still playing, regardless.

Elsewhere in the song he says, "I was born like this, I had no choice/I was born with the gift of a golden voice." One suspects he's also being tongue-in-cheek here. We remember Marty Machat saying to him, "If I want to hear a real singer I'll go to the Metropolitan Opera" and him not being in any way offended by the remark.

"Tower of Song" is almost like a *resumé* of his career. He sits like W.B. Yeats in another tower in Ireland, master of all he surveys. Just as we're expecting the album to get serious he pulls the rug from under his own feet with a "dee-do-dum-dum" refrain bringing him back to where the rest of us mortals live. The lightness, as a result, is welcome.

Cohen worked hard on the album, spending almost two years getting it ready. The fact that he meant business is evident even from the first track, "First We Take Manhattan," an ostensibly military song that has undertones of going on musical tours, where cities also have to be "conquered." Cohen didn't take it too seriously. Asked once by an interviewer what he planned to do after he "took" the city, he replied, "There will be a lot of new parking meters."

Not everyone could get away with eating a banana on an album cover. It was so naff it worked. Because it was Cohen, a man who made naff respectable. He wouldn't have been allowed to in the sixties when the Cool Gang were threatening his stature in the business. That was the thing about longevity. He liked to say, "Success is survival." If you sat long enough by the river you'd see the bodies of your enemies floating by.

The title song at first appears to be a seductive number *a la* Andrew Marvell's "To His Coy Mistress" but upon reflection it comes across more like a desperate attempt to re-ignite a love affair. It's a playful song, as Cohen no doubt was well aware of. He changed some of the words in certain concerts I attended. It was like Elvis used to do with "Are You Lonesome Tonight" in his later years.

"A man never got a woman back/ by begging on his knees," he sings, but that's what he does all the way through the song - irresistibly. He's like a Woody Allen figure here, poking fun at the big subjects - sex and death. It's as if he's finally gotten over the heaviness of his earlier years. Becoming more Groucho Marx than Ingmar Bergman, he's thrown away the philosopher's stone.

After all the decades of being the patron saint of lovesick lonely hearts, the so-called "bard of the bedsit" has now morphed into a kind of holy fool. The time had come to throw out the navel fluff and laugh in its face. The doom-and-gloom prophet bas become replaced by a prankster. His friends had always been aware of this side of him. "They think I'm a ball of laughs," he once said - unconvincingly. Now we were all seeing evidence of it.

His voice sounds huskier than usual on *I'm Your Man*. It's become a thousand cigarettes (or a thousand kisses?) deep. The album is also high calibre in the production department. He wrote the songs on a synthesiser, finding this to be more comfortable than using his guitar for them.

Listeners reacted warmly to the fact that he seemed to be taking himself less seriously than before. Tanita Tikaram even became a fan. In the old days, she said, he used to look like Dustin Hoffman and sing like Bob Dylan. Now he was getting "rather good at being Leonard Cohen." Cohen himself quipped, "I used to be a restless young man. Now I'm a restless middle-aged one."

"Ain't No Cure For Love" was another controversial song on the album. The title was inspired by a comment he made to Jennifer Warnes one day when they were out walking together during the AIDS epidemic in 1984.

She remarked of the enforced chastity imposed by the disease, "This is terrible. What are people going to do?" Cohen replied, "Well, honey, there ain't no cure for love." [5]

It was one of his hobbyhorse themes, the idea of love being, as Bob Dylan says in his song, "a four-lettered word." "Nobody can tolerate the ache of separation," he once said, "or the vertigo of surrender, but that doesn't mean we're going to abandon the whole deal."

This, he contended, was what the song was about. The going up, in other words, was worth the corning down - even if love, as Amy Winehouse would write some years down the line, was "a losing game."

The album made him "hot" again. He became listened to by people who didn't even know who he was before he made it.

He attributed his new-found popularity to the cyclical nature of the music business. In the sixties, he speculated, people discovered they had minds and sought out songs to suit.

After they became tired of this they decided they wanted to exercise their bodies instead, which ushered in an era of dumbed-down dance music. Then they got tired dancing and reverted back to the "thoughtful" music again.

He dedicated the album to Dominique Issermann. Gabriela Valenzuela claimed he'd promised to dedicate it to her. He'd been alternating between the two women for years.

Valenzuela thought she got the thin end of the stick by him, that she'd been kept hidden by him, unlike Issermann, who he was happy to talk to the media about and be seen out with.

In general she felt badly treated by Cohen, having to abort a baby of his she was carrying as well. She was also airbrushed out of all his biographies, including Sylvie Simmons' so-called definitive one, *I'm Your Man.*

There were many other women in his life around this time, women like Ann Diamond and Linda Clark who didn't generally feature in media reports about him.

Clark was one of his lovers from the late eighties. She said he always called his women "Darling" because he had so many of them he couldn't remember their names. She thought he had little trouble getting them. All he had to say at parties was something like "I'll be upstairs if anyone wants to join me." Sometimes his pursuit of women was fetishistic.

One night at a party in Montreal he took a strand from the hair of a woman who attracted him, dipped it in a glass of wine and then sucked it dry.

Clark saw Cohen as a case of arrested development. She believed he was formed by his mother in a way that was common with any Jewish men. They often had intimacy issues, she maintained,

119

because if women got too close, they felt they were being swallowed up in the same way. Cohen, she said, was "an over-oedipalized matriarchal man." This meant that whenever he was with a woman he felt he was betraying her in some way.

This strain was evidenced in its most extreme form in Alfred Hitchcock's film *Psycho* where the "mother" part of the main character, played by Anthony Perkins, makes him kill the woman he's attracted to (Janet Leigh).

There was also a corollary to this. The fact of being subjugated to his mother - Masha used to tie the young Leonard to a chair when she was cutting his hair - made him seek control of the women he met when he grew up.

Clark wasn't inclined to speak highly of Cohen after they broke up. Some of her pronouncements on him verge on the farcical. "Leonard puts a woman on a pedestal until she leaves the top of the toothpaste tube off," she accused, "and that's the end of that." [6]

Gale Zoe Garnett, another lover, tried to explain his complexities: "He wasn't faithful but he was loyal. If you were his friend you were his friend for life but if you betrayed him you were his enemy for life. It was easy to love him. Falling in love with him was the idiot act." His phrase, "I have been faithful to thee in my fashion," alludes to this streak in him.

He was usually hyper-sensitive to women's moods but if a relationship wasn't working for him he could be brutal in the ending of it. He felt he had to be. Too many other experiences awaited him.

He admitted he wasn't a good candidate for any kind of long term relationship with a woman. Elrod made him cynical about them. He got a lot of harsh treatment from her after they separated. She kept taking him to court for more money despite having got the children and the house in France.

When he told her he didn't have it, she accused him of being over-generous with his friends and Roshi, to whom he gave, she alleged, "huge donations." In between bouts of extorting money from him he was amused to see her reading the works of the 15th century Indian poet, Kabir. "Perfumed soap and a little Kabir," he wrote in a poem, "another hundred thousand and a little Kabir/A new stone house, a swimming pool/arguments, debts and facials/And here is Kabir's love swing."

Issermann broke it off with him after she discovered he'd cheated on her, but they remained friends. He continued to use her photographs of him on promotional material.

She wasn't sore with him, realising he wasn't a one-woman man. That was one of the reasons he never married. The hippies may have disowned him as a "square" at the end of the sixties but he shared their feelings about open relationships.

Issermann had provided solace to Cohen throughout the lean years of the eighties when his career had been going through rough patches. It was magnanimous of her to forgive him. Other women in similar predicaments didn't, leading to his pronouncement, "There is a war between the man and the woman."

In the absence of being involved in an actual war, the battle of the sexes became a quotidian substitute for him.

He readied himself for the challenge with each new partner, each new conquest, rebooting his mind if he got in too deep and he had to fight the deprivation. Or if he did and he had, to fight the guilt. In most cases he was in the driving seat but even then he carried battle scars.

121

They hardened him for the next abrasion, the next nicking away at that complicated heart. Each affair both strengthened and weakened him hut it was the only way he could play it.

Permanence, or the threat of it, was always a much greater fear for him than loneliness.

Cohen's childhood home on Belemont Avenue.

Cohen on television in the 1960s at the start of his career.

Leonard in 1988.

1988.

Cohen back on tour.

Cohen in Denmark in 2013

Dublin Visit

I wasn't an instant convert to Cohen. The first singers I listened to seriously were Bob Dylan and Elvis. Dylan "owned" the sixties. Elvis went soft in that decade. John Lennon famously said, "Elvis died the day he went into the army." Dylan was the guy who was "doing it" after Elvis sold out to Hollywood.

I went to America for the summer of 1972. I was in university at the time and we got long holidays. My brother Basil was staying in a house in Connecticut. He said I could stay with him. I couldn't get a job for the first few weeks over there.

It was a lazy time. I didn't do much except sit around and play records. The one I had on the turntable most often was "More Bob Dylan Greatest Hits." It was a double album Basil had. I almost wore the needle out. One of the other people in the house couldn't stand him. "He can't sing!" he'd scream out every time I put the record on. That only made me more interested in playing it.

I visited America again in 1973. Dylan had just appeared in the film *Pat Garret and Billy the Kid*. He was no actor but he had a certain presence as 'Alias,' his well-named character. The album wasn't great either, apart from the stunning "Knockin' at Heaven's Door,' which I was hooked on.

I also liked *New Morning*, another album of his that came out that year, and *Self-Portrait*, a double album that most people I knew hated.

After I came home to Ireland I met Mary, the woman who would eventually become my wife. We had a shared interest in music. I talked to her a lot about Dylan's pugnacious attitude to life.

"I prefer Leonard Cohen," she insisted. His work was only vaguely familiar to me then.

"What about Dylan?" I said. She said she liked him but Cohen hit her at a part of herself that Dylan couldn't.

She played some of his songs for me. I was impressed by them but he was a slow-burning fuse for me then. Being a university student, I was into high energy singers with "attitude."

I loved the way Dylan spat out his songs. His tone as much as his words screamed Angry Young Man. Cohen looked so civilised in comparison.

How could you be a rebel when you dressed in a suit? Cohen was also nearly thirty. Like most university students of the time I was ageist. How arrogant we were then.

My devotion to Cohen wasn't "love at first sound" as it had been with Elvis and Dylan. It took me a while to get to like his songs in the way Mary did.

She played them over and over and eventually won me round. When she did, there was no going back.

Mary loved all Cohen's songs but especially *Famous Blue Raincoat.* We used to play this on the record player in her house in Artane sitting on the carpet.

She thought it was the best song he ever wrote - in fact the best song anyone ever wrote. The line "A flake of your life" spoke to her particularly.

Mary had met Irving Layton in 1969 in the Aran Islands and he took a shine to her,

even wrote a poem for her. He wrote it on the back of a cigarette packet and typed it out that evening in his boarding house, presenting it to her the following day. It went like this:

131

SONG FOR MARY

Willie Yeats had his Maude Gonne;
I have Mary Mannion
Who is as fair as the dawn.

Though her eyes are grey
As the break of day,
They are warm and gay.

The years will never chase
The beauty from her face
Or from her form its quiet grace.

I have come from a far land
That I may touch her hand.
O bury me in an Irish strand.

Irving Layton
Aran
July 23, 1969

It was bucketing rain on the night of the concert. After we entered the stadium we were aware of an almost reverential hush, the hush of a gathering about to witness the arrival of some kind of Messiah. We sat at the foot of the stage as the lights went down. There was silence for a few moments. Then we saw a figure coming onto the stage. He didn't look at us, only down at his guitar.

Neither did he introduce himself. He just plucked a few strings on the guitar. Then he started singing. The song, perhaps inevitably, was "Suzanne." In no time at all we were all singing along with him.

I saw him as being like a rabbi on an altar, a man who looked as if he'd be happy singing to himself even if we weren't there, throwing his words out to the air like a sailor searching for a port, maybe, or someone putting them into a bottle to be washed up on some far-distant shore.

After he finished the song we clapped. It wasn't rapturous applause but it was sustained. He thanked us profusely as if it was a surprise to him. For the next two hours he sang most of his best known songs. He didn't soup them up or make any special pleading for them. We didn't expect him to and he seemed to know that. They spoke for themselves. He didn't sell them, or himself, because he didn't need to.

We sang along to "So Long, Marianne," "Tonight Will Be Fine," "Sisters of Mercy." Most of us seemed to know the words to them. Now and then we drowned him out. In some ways it was like sitting on the carpet in Artane listening to him on the record player. I found it difficult to work up the enthusiasm I expected to have.

The size of the venue, which wasn't quite full, and the wicked night, conspired against that. But when he sang "Famous Blue Raincoat,"

133

the song I'd been waiting for all night, I felt transported into another world.

The song he chose to close the show was "Chelsea Hotel." After he finished it he said it was about a woman who was no longer alive. "Ignore her story at your peril," he said before going offstage.

The concert was over. Just like that. We didn't stamp our feet to entice him back. Maybe we thought that would be too vulgar for such a refined performer. I looked at the dazed expressions of the people around me, wondering if they were excited or disappointed. Which experience was Mary feeling? She didn't say.

We filtered out of the stadium into the cold and the rain, back to our bedsits. We'd seen Leonard Cohen live. Pinch yourself.

I was writing some articles for *In Dublin* magazine at this time. By day I was a teacher but I was finding the job difficult. I was hoping I could get out of it and make a living by writing. *In Dublin* was one of my first attempts to bring this about.

I rang the editor the following morning. He knew I was going to the concert. "What did you think of it?" he asked me. I told him it was brilliant. We discussed me writing a review of it. Then he said, "Would you like to interview him? If you would, we can arrange it." It was, as Don Corleone might have said, an offer I couldn't refuse.

He set it up. The next day I made my way to Jury's hotel, which was where he was staying. I had a hundred questions in my head to ask him but feared corpsing when it came time to ask them. When I got to the hotel I was expecting to be surrounded by dozens of journalists but I found myself sitting alone in a corridor waiting to be summoned in to him. The hype from *I'm Your Man* hadn't kicked in yet. He was still "That guy from the sixties who sings all those doleful songs."

Eventually one of his PR women came out of a room. "He's ready," she said. I went in, taking my seat at a table. A few moments later he swept in. I thought he looked a bit like a mafia don: grey suit, greying hair, almost effeminate in his courtliness as he greeted me.

His handshake was warm, his smile affable. One of his minders waved his hand at him with some fingers raised, presumably gesturing the time I was going to be allotted. He nodded at him before going out. The door closed. I was alone with my hero.

I went through the set of questions I intended to ask him. A lot of them seemed silly suddenly. I'd just bought a tape recorder, one of those little ones that held cassettes. I wasn't sure of that either. He seemed amused watching me fiddling with it, trying to get it on "Record."

I apologised. He chuckled. "You don't mind me using this, do you?" I said, "My memory isn't the best." He chuckled again. "Mine neither," he said. I severely doubted that considering the words of all the songs he had to remember at his concerts. Maybe it was easier when you'd written them yourself.

I turned on the recorder. "I suppose you're used to these things being pushed under your face," I said. I told him I'd just bought it the day before and didn't totally trust myself to operate it properly. He said, "I'm also used to them not working."

The spool spun around in the machine. It made a dull crackle. He looked at me, waiting for my first question. I cleared my throat. My tongue felt thick in my mouth. I wanted to tell him that he made me the person I was, for better or worse, that I owed him a huge debt for all the years I'd spent marvelling at his words. But of course that wouldn't have been professional. I had to forget the fact that I was a fan.

I told him I'd seen him at the stadium. "I love that place," he said, his voice seeming to come from the bowels of the earth.

I asked him how it felt to be back in the limelight with his new album. "It's nice when they're applauding," he said, "When they're not, you have to figure out what to do with the silence." Then he said an unusual thing: "I never thought I was God."

I told him we hadn't been hearing too much about him in Ireland in recent times. He said, "They haven't been hearing too much about me anywhere else either!"[1]

Did it bother him that people spoke of him as a depressing writer? "Sometimes you get tagged for something that you don't think you are. It gets into the computer and one generation of journalists after the other keep repeating it to you. You just have to put up with it."

I told him I didn't agree with that perception of him. "There's nothing as depressing as bad comedy," I said. "That's good," he said smiling. He smiled as much with his eyes as his mouth. He'd said something similar himself some years before: "We can be destroyed by mindless frivolity as surely as by obsessive depression." [2]

I started to feel relaxed. He settled back in his chair. Maybe if I could just chat to him instead of interviewing him, I thought, I'd get more out of him.

He talked a bit about how it was for him starting out, how people were against him even before they'd listened to him. It was frustrating dealing with negative publicity that was unfounded.

How was he with criticism in general? "If it's fair I'll take it on board. If it isn't I'll probably ignore it." Was it hard to do that? "Not really. I've been in this racket so long I''ve developed a thick skin."

I asked him if the idea of being a Jew in a French quarter of Montreal gave him a sense of being schizoid. Did the mixture of influences make him in any way confused about where he stood on religious or political issues?

He furrowed his brow, sitting forward in the chair. "I have a lot of conflicts," he said, "I'm a hopeless political animal because I feel attracted to so many positions that can't be reconciled. I love the conservative point of view but also the radical subversive one. I love the ideals of family, church, honour, integrity and tribe but also the idea of anarchy, free love, cosmopolitanism, internationalism. Libertinism conflicts with my deep sense of order. A part of me believes everything should be in its place and another part believes nothing should have a place."[3] I was amazed at how he had all these words at will, at how he could churn them out.

Perhaps because I was Irish he talked to me about his love for Yeats. I said I thought he shared a sense of transience with him. "In the morning we spout as flowers," he said, "In the evening we are cut down and withereth. Therefore teach us to number our days."

I put it to him that Yeats' rejection in love by Maud Gonne MacBride was said to have bequeathed a great legacy of poetry to the world. Did he believe great literature came from suffering? He said, "Not exclusively. I think it comes from both suffering and other parts of us. Yeats is complex because he's a modern man. A modern man has to deal with a sense of loss."[4]

Next to Lorca he said Yeats was his favourite poet. He talked about how he started reading them, how they moved him so much. "I wanted to be a writer instead of a singer," he said, "but after finishing two novels that failed to sell 1 realised I could never make a living from it."

Was it true that the discovery of Lorca's poetry set him on his way to being a writer? "I don't know. He definitely ignited something in

137

my heart, some kind of possibility. He invoked a landscape I was always living in but didn't know about. No other poet had done that to me at the time. I was forced to read Shakespeare and he didn't do it to me. Lorca and Yeats were the two poets who touched me the most."

I thought I should talk to him about his album. Did he really believe there was no cure for love? He sidestepped the question: "I sometimes believe I'm dying of this incurable disease called age!. No, there's no cure for anything." Was writing an answer? "It's one. Alcohol is another. Austerity is another response, promiscuity another. It drives everybody crazy."

I asked him about the two Suzannes in his life, the one who was the subject of his song and the one who was the mother of Adam and Lorca. At that time I was confused between the two. He must have been bored talking about the difference between them to people but he did so again now. He explained that he met the mother of his children long after he wrote about the other one, who was married to a friend of his.

Were the circumstances of the song based on fact?

"She lived down by the St. Lawrence river at the Montreal harbour. There's a Seaman's Club out over it so all the landmarks are concrete." Was a lot of his work autobiographical in this way? "A large part is reportage." I liked the way he said "reportage" with the French inflection.

He talked about religion, about how it should play a part in people's lives even if God didn't exist. I thought this was an unusual thing to say. He said it was important for people's well-being, for the well-being of society in general. "Religion is a stabiliser," he said, "If God doesn't exist, we'd have to invent him, as they say. There are no atheists in foxholes. I would probably subscribe to the idea that the person who searches for God has already found him."

In the song "Who By Fire," who did he think was calling? "Whatever the energy is. The shadow or what's behind the shadow. We're continually being summoned, continually rising and continually being sown."[5]

Did he believe that only drowning men could see Jesus like he said in the song? Was it important to go down on one's knees to achieve redemption?

"I think you have to surrender, and surrendering often involves going down on your knees, or on your back or on your belly. In those moments you have to forget about the things that held you up. You have to let them go. When you do that, something comes into your heart that's your true mainstay. Your deepest resources are called into activity then."[6]

We got onto the subject of where his inspiration originated. I was familiar with his statement, "If I knew where the good songs came from, I'd go there more often." He'd said it to a number of people in interviews. Was he aware of where that place was now? "You never know," he said, "The more you look for it, the less chance you have of finding it. I work hard at what I do but sometimes I think that comes against me. I've often spent hours trying to fix a line of a song or a verse of a poem that isn't right without getting anywhere. Then I go away from it and something completely different from it triggers the answer to my problem."

I asked him if he ever felt that when he wrote a song, it was actually lying in wait for him before he discovered it. I was thinking of a sculptor who once said though his statues were inside the slabs of stone he broke. He said he'd never thought of it that way but it was

139

an interesting concept. If it was true it would give him "more faith in the process."

In her creative novel *The Water and the Wine*, author Tamar Hodes has Cohen saying to Marianne about his writing, "I am beholden to it. I am not the master. I am the servant. It controls me."[7]

This idea taps into the notion I put to him about his works possibly preceding him and him discovering them. Rilke liked to say, "I'm sure there are many books that must long for the deaths of their authors so they can take on a life of their own."

He had a reputation for being painstaking in the writing of his songs. How true was this perception of him? "I believe in patience and perseverance. If you hang in there long enough, they're going to yield. Often you're not in charge of that. You keep your tools sharpened, you keep yourself in the kind of shape necessary to be able to work, you learn tricks over the years to keep yourself going, but eventually the deep places have to speak on their own. You summon things from places you don't command."

Did that mean he was a victim of them? "I don't know if victim is the right word." Was he a receptacle? "Yes. You're a receptacle."

I asked him how he felt about Jennifer Warnes' *Famous Blue Raincoat* album. He said it had been especially helpful in re-establishing his credibility in America. How did it come about? "I've known her since she was in diapers. She sang back-up for me as far back as 1972. She's always been saying she wanted to do an album of my songs. I thought it was just an expression of friendship but she really meant it."

Was it difficult to get off the ground? "She went from one record company to another and they laughed her out of their offices. They said the last thing the world needed was a record by Leonard Cohen. But she eventually found a small company to do it."[8]

Did he like how she sang his songs? "She's got one of these voices where every moment of sound is equally agreeable." He said he thought she should have been more successful than she was, that it got her down sometimes that she wasn't. "I always said to her, 'Don't worry, just keep recording, do a record every year to keep your name out there - classic, country and western, anything.' Because she can bring real life to any kind of song. She has that gift."[9]

I told him I thought she made a fabulous job of the album, especially the title song. He agreed. "It's a difficult one to sing," he said, "even for me."

I said it had always confused me. He said he didn't really know what it was about either. There was a time he did but not now. He "changed a few pronouns" in it recently. If he was writing it today, he thought, he'd make it clearer. I said I didn't think that would be a good idea, that the magic lay in the mystery. He thanked me for that. I said my basic understanding of it was that it concerned a man who almost stole his lover. Was that the gist of it? "It's a kind of impressionist painting of jealousy," he said, "of the evolution of jealousy into generosity."

The PR woman came in again. She looked at him as if to say my time was up but he ignored her. He talked about how difficult it was to attract audiences at the beginning of his singing career. "I thought they hated me. I had no confidence in myself. I seriously considered giving it all up and going back to my writing."

Were we due a collection of poetry soon? "I've been blackening some pages. I hope to sift through it pretty soon. When you're on the road it's hard to think of much beyond the next concert."

141

What did he see as the difference between a poem and a song? "It's hard to say. There are certain technical differences. Poems usually move more slowly. When you write a poem you can stop. You can pause on a line and go back. The thing is perceived in a time frame. A song, on the contrary, has to move swiftly from beat to beat. There has to be a lot of space around the words because otherwise it's too confusing. In my own case I never had a strategy. I never knew what I was doing most of the time. I still don't."[10]

His bewilderment didn't surprise me. I'd read somewhere that he said, "I have no programme. I just move from hotel to hotel and bar to bar. By the grace of the one above, occasionally a song comes."[11]

Elsewhere he'd said, "I can never figure out the kind of tie to put on in the morning. I don't have a plan to get through the day. It's literally a problem for me to decide which side of the bed to get out of."[12]

He once described his songwriting process as being "about as graceful as a bear trying to get honey out of a highly populated beehive." This sounded more like Bob Dylan than himself. Was it more difficult to write a song than a poem? "People sometimes accuse me of doing the same thing in both forms. I'm at pains to explain to them that I don't. If one turns into the other it's an accident."

Would he agree that he put his talent into his songs and his genius into his poetry?

He paused for a few moments before answering this. Eventually he said, "They say there are three categories: talent, genius and divinity. Divinity takes all notions of the strategy of composition away."

Who had it?

"People like Rimbaud, Picasso."

Did it help Picasso's art in his view?

"He's always shining with some kind of energy that doesn't refer to anything. It's just smashing away at its own limits. If you've got divinity, it doesn't matter if you can draw a straight line or not."

But surely, I suggested, Picasso mastered representational art before he went into cubism. Was it important to be a good conservative before one became a good radical?

He looked as if things were getting a bit too opaque for him. Maybe, he speculated, one should just be "a good boy!"

He talked about his years in Hydra, saying it was his bolthole from the deadening cities where he plied his trade. I asked him how he spent his time there. It was a stupid question. We were running out of time and I was asking him to describe five years in a few sentences. "I drank," he said, "I wrote a few songs, went through a few families."

Marianne, of course, was the reason he stayed there for so many years. After spending most of the sixties with her, he said, he left her for his other life, that of the writer-cum-singer in America. He sent her tickets for his concerts over the years but they were scant consolation to her: "She didn't take the parting well." The relationship had been so good between them she thought it was going to last forever but that wasn't possible for him: "My mind was elsewhere."

The PR woman appeared again. This time I knew she meant business by the look on her face. There was so much more I wanted to ask him but I couldn't. "Maybe you'll come back here some other time," I hazarded. "Many times, I hope," he said. Nobody could ever have known then that the number of times would run into double figures.

He stood up. I thanked him for his time and wished him well with the rest of his tour. He shook my hand again. Before I left I handed him a collection of stories I'd written in 1980.

I don't know why. It wasn't a particularly good one. Mary's Irving Layton poem would have been more appropriate but at that time I didn't even know he knew Layton.

"This looks very nice," he said. "I'll read it when I can." As I watched him going out the door I found myself hoping he wouldn't.

Burn-Out

Adam had a horrific car accident in 1990. He was working as a roadie for a calypso band in the Caribbean island of Guadeloupe at the time. He broke his neck and suffered other injuries to his ribs and his hip as well as puncturing his lung. He was flown by ambulance to Toronto and spent the next four months in a coma. Cohen rushed to be by his side. He spent most of the next year with him.

At one point the doctors weren't sure if he'd survive. They drilled holes in his forehead so they could put a helmet on his head to keep it still. Cohen was out of his mind with worry. Nothing else became important to him now except this. The accident brought the two of them closer than they'd ever been before.

When he finally came out of his coma, the first sound he heard was his father reading the Bible to him. He said, "Dad, can you read something else?"[1]

Cohen was inducted into the Canadian Hall of Fame that year. If it had happened to him when he was 26, he said, it might have turned his head. Likewise if he got it at 36 or 46. But at 56, "Hell, I'm just hitting my stride."[2]

A tribute album to him came out in 1991. Despite the purgatorial pun of the title (*I'm Your Fan*) it went down well with the public and had respectable sales.

Cohen began a relationship with the actress Rebecca De Mornay at this time. He'd been a friend of hers since the late 1980's when she lived near him in L.A. She was familiar with his music from childhood, her mother using it as a lullaby for her. She made her most well-known film in 1992, *The Hand That Rocks the Cradle*, playing a nanny from hell. She'd recently become separated from the scriptwriter Bruce Wagner. Cohen sent her three dozen yellow roses every day after they started dating.

He remembered seeing her as a five-year-old girl during a visit to the school in Suffolk that Axel attended in the mid-sixties, the progressive Summerhill establishment.

It was amazing that he was able to carry a memory for so long. He met her again in 1986 at a party in Robert Altman's house. Sparks flew between them that night. Their relationship became public when Cohen accompanied her to the Oscar ceremonies in 1992. Everyone was surprised to see him stepping out with her, especially since it was a non-musical event.

Cohen played down her "Hollywood superstar" aura. When band member Steve Zirkel first saw them together he said to her, "Did anybody ever tell you that you look like Rebecca De Mornay?" he went, "Who's that?" De Mornay was just as good. She went, "I get that a lot."

He was 25 years older than her, a fact that gave him some pause. "There's nothing more inappropriate than an old guy coming on," he quaked. But she didn't have a problem with the age gap.

There were riots in Los Angeles that year. Four police officers had been arrested for the brutal murder of Rodney King but were acquitted. He was a black man who'd been falsely accused of resisting arrest by them. Footage of them brutalising him was ignored. Cohen watched the city burning from the window of his house with a perverse fascination.

De Mornay couldn't understand why he lived there. He told her that even though it had decay in it, it also had "some kind of wild hope."[3] In a strange way it reminded him of himself. The chaos of the city, he maintained, "nourished" him. He liked it because of its desperation, adding that it was also the only city in the U.S. where he found he was able to write a song while sitting in a driveway in a parked car.[4]

He recorded another album that year, *The Future*. He was proud of it, telling an interviewer from MTV that it was as rigidly structured as a Sherman tank. The title track, with the line, "I have seen the future, baby, it is murder," was inspired - if that's the word - by the riots.

This song is Cohen's "A Hard Rain's A-Gonna Fall." It's infused with a dystopian sense that's undercut by the upbeat tempo. Otherwise it might have turned into what Bob Dylan used to call a "finger-pointing" song. Cohen tried to avoid these. He didn't want to be like Martin Luther, nailing manifestos to church doors.

Another song on the album, "Democracy," is the polar opposite of "The Future." Here the Malthusian message is undercut by Cohen's doggerel-like rhyming scheme. Does he really believe democracy is coming to the USA?

The tone seems too chirpy, especially for this man. If the negative lyrics of "The Future" are belied by the music, in "Democracy" the positive ones are. Cohen believed America was "the last best hope" for democracy in the world but he also said, "If voting changed anything, they'd probably make it illegal." How does one reconcile the two viewpoints. I can't see how. As he said to me, "I'm a useless political animal." Translated into English that means he was too honest to be one.

"Democracy" is more upbeat than most of Cohen's tracks but not as jingoistic as, say, Bruce Springsteen's "Born in the USA." At times it sounds more Scott Joplin than Janis. It was written after the fall of the Berlin Wall. Cohen didn't share the optimism of most people following that event. "What a surprise," he harumphed, "Me being grumpy about something."

Hence this number. He wrote so many verses for it, he said he could have filled the whole album with it. The lyrics are clever, perhaps too clever, leading to it sounding contrived at times. The marching rhythm he employed in so many of his songs is in evidence. It was more solemn in numbers like "First We Take Manhattan." Here it's almost frivolous, making us suspect an irony in the overt celebratory air of the song. Between the lines, we think, he could be saying something else. If democracy isn't in Berlin, neither is it totally in the USA according to Field Commander Cohen.

There's also an element of doggerel about "Closing Time." Here once again the dour title works against the rhythm to confuse us about its intent. Cohen is less ironic in the other tracks on the album – "Waiting for the Miracle," "Light as the Breeze" and the album's two covers, "Be For Real" and "Always."

The stand-out song on the album is "Anthem." Cohen believed this was one of the best songs he ever wrote. It's also the one that contains his most quoted phrase: "There is a crack in everything/That's how the light gets in."

People who don't know anything about him are probably familiar with these two lines. They've been quoted by everyone from priests to wellness counsellors to trendy people at cocktail parties who want to sound intelligent.

Why have they become so championed every time one brings up Cohen's name? Probably because of the confluence of frailty and catharsis they index. In this sense they're like a microcosm of his broken world. Even the famous blue raincoat is torn at the shoulder.

Michael Posner, who edited three volumes of oral histories relating to Cohen, believed he got the phrase from a Tibetan monk in a monastery in Scotland which he visited in 1969. After complaining about a broken shutter, the monk told him, "The crack is how the light gets in."[5] They could even be traced back to Native American culture where shamans were reputed to derive their power from cracked skulls through which supernatural powers could enter.[6]

The Irish author John McKenna had a friendship with Cohen that lasted over thirty years. He once sent him a poem called "Advent" by Patrick Kavanagh.

It has a speculation similar to Cohen's in "Anthem": "Through a chink too wide there comes in no wonder." McKenna thought some of Kavanagh's poems were up there with Yeats but Cohen was unflinching in his devotion to the older poet. For McKenna this was "a battle lost."[7] It's possible he hit a nerve with Cohen by suggesting this source for his most famous two lines, thereby impugning against his originality.

Cohen dedicated the album to De Mornay, thereby making it into a kind of unofficial revamp of the abandoned *Songs for Rebecca*. He also gave her a co-producer credit on it. This was a tokenistic gesture resulting from the amount of time she spent listening to him recording it. She decided on the final version of "Anthem" in the studio one day with the comment, "That's it!"

He'd worked hard on the song but, like "Democracy" (if not all the ones he wrote) he had trouble finishing it, or recognising when he sang it best. De Mornay was better able to judge this from a distance, which led to him accepting her superior judgment. Apart from this, her right to have a producer credit on the album remains

149

dubious. She'd written a few songs in her past, according to Cohen, but had no experience in production until she met him.

He did a series of concerts to promote the album. They were popular with audiences, with lots of celebrities in attendance. Kurt Cobain visited him one night in his dressing room after a show. Bill Clinton even asked for "Democracy" to be played at his inauguration. He'd just been elected president.

Cohen appeared at a concert in Barcelona in May 1993 at which he looked the worse for wear. An excerpt from it appeared on the DVD *Leonard Cohen: The Live Broadcast Sessions, 1985-1993*. The heavy workload of touring that began with the release of *I'm Your Man* seemed evident. Maybe that was what "the road" did with singers. The following month, however, he performed a fantastic concert at the O'Keeffe Centre in Toronto. His 7-minute version of "Bird on the Wire" at this concert ranks as my all-time favourite rendition of the song by him.

He was drinking a lot at this time, sometimes up to three bottles of wine a day. Touring led to things like that. He was knocked out of his ordinary routines and plonked into ones dictated by "the road." It was a case of airports, hotel rooms and concerts, singing the same songs in different cities every other night, a mixture of repetition and variety that did his head in.

He compared it to being dropped off in a desert: "You don't know where you live anymore or if you still have a car or a girlfriend or a wife and kids." He had a car and a girlfriend and kids all right, but the likelihood of a wife was anyone's guess.

He was getting on well with De Mornay at this time. Some people speculated that he might "go the distance" with her. They were actually engaged to be married at one stage. He'd been engaged to

Elrod too. It seemed to be something he did with women to stop them leaving him. Was it a kind of holding strategy he didn't intend to deliver on?

De Mornay conducted a fun interview with him in 1993. She began by saying she liked the idea of doing so because it meant she could be sure she wouldn't be asked the question, "What is the nature of your relationship with Leonard Cohen?" Without batting an eye, Cohen jumped in with, "I'd like to know. Let's start with that question!"[8]

They broke up shortly afterwards. Apparently she wanted to get married and have children. Neither prospect appealed to Cohen. As was the case with the character in her most famous film, she wasn't destined to "rock the cradle" for a while yet.

They remained friends after they separated. Cohen thanked her for, as he put it, letting him "off the hook." [9] Asked why they broke up, he grinned, "She got wise to me."[10]

Losing her depressed him. Many lovers he'd had in the past were content to inhabit the limbo in which he placed them, neither committing to anything long term nor letting go. De Mornay was different. He found it hard to deal with that. He'd got in deep with her. After she left him he went to pieces, drowning his sorrows in wine.

Perla Batalla, one of his backing singers, sent him a letter after he parted from her. It contained a clipping from a San Francisco magazine which featured an ad from a woman looking for a man with "the passion of Leonard Cohen and the rawness of Iggy Pop." He told Iggy about it, which resulted in the two men meeting up and having their photo taken together. Cohen sent it to the woman who put in the ad.

151

The album *Cohen Live* was released in 1994. It contained footage of many of his concert performances from 1988 to 1993. "My voice deepened during these years," he informed the media, "thanks to 50,000 cigarettes." The poet Charles Bukowski died in the March of that year. Cohen had been an unlikely fan of his work. "He brought everyone down," he jibed, "including the angels."

The two of them couldn't have been more different. One of them dressed well, was unfailingly courteous to people and didn't get drunk in public. The other delighted in disgracing himself and being confrontational with most of the people he met.

Cohen admired Bukowski. In some ways he reminded him of Irving Layton. They were both larger-than-life souls who delighted in tilting at windmills.

Another outrageous talent, Kurt Cobain, overdosed the following month. Cohen had heard he was depressed and addicted to various substances. He thought he might have been able to help him if he got to him in time. This was unlikely. Despite having visited him that night after his concert, Cobain wasn't a fan of his work. He found it depressed him. It didn't take a genius to work out that Cohen's music wouldn't be "good medicine" for anyone on the amount of drugs Cobain was.

Cohen was aware he could go down the road travelled by Bukowski and Cobain if he didn't hit the "Pause" button on his life. He needed to, as it were, quell his "swollen appetite."

As well as drinking too much, he was also taking a lot of pills. One night a pharmacist refused to give him some of the ones he asked him for. An unusually cranky Cohen rasped, "Are you afraid I'm going to knock off gas stations?"[11]

The medication he'd been given in the early nineties did him more harm than good. It was meant to stabilise his moods but it left him unable to leave his bed or his house. He described himself vividly when he said, "I was living in an aquarium full of cotton wool."[12]

It was time to do something radical. He knew what that had to be. In the autumn of 1993 he drove up to a Zen Buddhist retreat 6500 metres above the ground called Mount Baldy and signed himself in. He'd been going there on retreats for years. This time he intended to stay for a much longer time.

It was a good time for him to try and turn his life around. He also wanted to re-connect with Roshi. He hadn't been seeing much of him in recent times. De Mornay hadn't got on with him. He was in his nineties now. Cohen felt he mightn't live long more.

The timing of the move to Mount Baldy was right for himself too. He'd just reached sixty. A book came out to mark the occasion. *Take This Waltz: A Celebration of Leonard Cohen* was a collection of tributes to him in prose and verse. There were contributions from such luminaries as Kris Kristofferson, Jack McClelland, Joan Baez, Allen Ginsberg, Judy Collins and many more. They all wrote about him with great feeling.

Fan David McFadden put it best of all when he said, "Leonard Cohen, I see you as an exotic extra-terrestrial who is just visiting (earth). You're a native of an unimaginably strange and remote little planet from which few souls venture forth except on special missions which are inexplicable in human terms. There are many Leonard Cohens on that planet. On this there is only one."[13]

He was now about to go to a different kind of world, one that was on the earth but not of it. After forty years of hard work he felt he was entitled to find some stability for himself. "It's your time," Adam told him, "Go for it."

Lorca had just come through that difficult teenage phase most parents had to suffer: funky clothes, "attitude" and rings on every available aperture on her body. Both she and Adam were in their twenties now. They didn't need him to be around them as much as before. Time had matured them. They were about to make their own way in life. Cohen felt able to say to them, and to the world, as Frank Sinatra had in the 1970s when he began his first retirement, "Excuse me while I disappear."

Some people thought he was entering the monastery to repent for his wild life. He didn't see it like that. He told his friends he just needed to recharge his batteries. For some time now he'd been running on empty. Another reason he was feeling poorly at this time was because Esther's husband Victor had just died. He said to his fellow monk Eric Lerner one night, "I can't stand people anymore."[14]

Mount Baldy spared him all the stress that had been part and parcel of his life for too many years now, the stress of having to deal with executives, women, even fans. All these were going to be absent from his new life.

The idea of someone in the music business opting for a monastic lifestyle threw many people. The contrast to his outside life was too great for them to comprehend. He found it hard to convince them that he'd never been fully a part of that other world. Entering the monastery, in some ways, felt like going home.

He shovelled snow on most days. Afterwards there was meditation, exchanging pleasantries with the other monks. He also spent some time carrying boulders from place to place. This wasn't a problem for him. In fact he enjoyed it, the physical activity freeing his mind from the detritus it had built up from all the years of dealing with mercenary boneheads from "Boogie Street."

Sitting in a room in the middle of nowhere - or rather on top of it – didn't make him feel as isolated as being in one in Los Angeles with a beer and a TV set for company. He said he felt more alone in the teeming masses of L.A. than in the monastery. That was because of the fellow feeling he experienced with the other monks. He compared them to pebbles in a bag, polishing one another.[15]   It was a contrast to the "tyrannical solitude" of city life.[16]

It should be noted that Cohen was no ordinary monk. He was one with privileges. Kelley Lynch's father had renovated his cabin. Lynch had become his manager after Marty Machat died in 1988.

He installed a computer and a bathtub - and even a synthesiser. Cohen also had a library, and alcohol. This wasn't quite going back to nature. It was more a "rus in urbe" retreat where he knew his eardrums wouldn't be pummelled by the noise of someone screaming next door, as he often experienced in the Chelsea Hotel, or even someone overdosing. From this point of view it was "the perfect hotel room."

An open regime existed at the monastery. Some of the monks got married. A few of them drank. Roshi was capable of calling someone in from shovelling snow at 6 a.m. to join him in a glass of cognac. Affairs were even accepted between the monks and any women who were around. "If you want to fall in love with a beautiful young nun," Cohen told an interviewer, "Go ahead." All that was demanded was that one "suffered sufficiently." He was doing that.[17]

But could he really describe such a place as a "spiritual retreat"? "I'm not here to recapture spiritual feelings so much as to discover them," he explained, "It's only people who aren't religious who have to pray." Elsewhere he said he was in Mount Baldy to get *away* from God.[18] He could say anything he wanted about these matters, couldn't he? He was, after all, the little Jew who wrote the Bible.

He generally rose at 2.30 a.m. even though he didn't have to be up until 3. The reason was to fortify him with coffee, "without which I wouldn't have been able to face the day."

He then put on his "absurd" robes and cooked breakfast for Roshi. There was a retreat every fourth week where he sat meditating for 18 hours a day, "like the other freaks." It was, he surmised, "a life designed to overthrow you."[19]

Even so, it was better than a health farm to him. On health farms, he pointed out, you didn't get an opportunity to bang nails and carry boulders.[20] Neither did you get the opportunity to meditate. Ironically, this proved to be more physically debilitating to him than carrying the boulders. He claimed to have worn out the cartilages in his knees from sitting cross-legged with the other monks.

The poet David Salway castigated Cohen for what he described as his "flirtation" with Buddhism in Mount Baldy. To his mind it clashed with his Jewishness. The "navel-gazing" Cohen experienced in Zen was annoying to Salway. To his mind it was antithetical to the rigid belief structure of the Jewish religion. Cohen didn't see a problem in embracing contrasting ideologies. "I have a perfectly good religion," he said, "Zen doesn't affect it in the least."

He described himself as a "pseudo-Buddhist." By this he meant that it was simply something to help him with "the mechanics of living." One night when he was eating a smoked-meat sandwich and drinking wine, his friend Lou Pomanti said he didn't think Buddhist monks did that. Cohen replied, "I'm a Buddhist when it's appropriate."

Neither did he see himself as having given up his career when he became a monk. He said he was just taking a break from it. Kelley Lynch kept his music going when he was in Mount Baldy just like "Colonel" Tom Parker did for Elvis Presley when he was in the army.

1993 saw the release of *Stranger Music,* an anthology of his verse and songs. Lynch also brought out *Cohen Live,* an album featuring concerts from the previous two years. Other things were happening too. Oliver Stone featured a number of songs from *The Future* in his film *Natural Born Killers* in 1994. This gave Cohen some much-needed exposure to younger listeners. He hadn't had much of that for some years now.

A tribute album, *Tower of Song,* came out in 1995. The novelist Tom Robbins wrote the liner notes, going into something of a purple patch as he described Cohen as having "a voice raked by the claws of Cupid, a voice rubbed raw by the philosopher's stone, a voice marinated in kirschwasser, sulfur, deer musk and snow, a penitent's voice, a rabbinical voice, a voice like a carpet in an old hotel, like a bad itch on the hunchback of love." Nobody, Robbins added, could use the word "naked" as powerfully as he. (Joni Mitchell agreed, but she thought he made it sound vulgar).

Cohen became an ordained Zen monk on August 9, 1996, taking the name Jikan. It meant "Silent One." To Roshi it suggested he was there for the long haul but no sooner had he given this formal commitment to his new lifestyle than he contemplated leaving it.

He spent three further years there but he didn't seem to have his heart in it. It was as if it had performed its function by cleaning him out and ridding him of the demons he'd accumulated during all the years of touring. One day he hung his robes on a peg and made the

157

long journey back to the outside world, telling himself at every step: "I am not a spiritual person."

This, of course, was nonsense. He just wasn't cut out for the 24/7 discipline a monastic life demanded. He described the years in Mount Baldy as being similar to scraping rust off one's soul. Maybe the Betty Ford clinic did something similar for less hieratic celebrities

Why did he choose this particular time to leave? Maybe the fact that Roshi was still healthy was a factor. If he was ill he couldn't have left him. The fact that he was in rude health at his great age posed a different kind of problem for Cohen. If he lived a long time more it might be too late for him to get back to his career.

He told Eric Lerner he left because "I'm not able to breathe anymore." The cure for his old life had become worse than the life itself.

Whatever his reasons, he seemed to be looking forward to going back to the world he'd left behind him. "I've come down from the mountain," he told documentary film-maker Harry Rasky, "A great weight has been lifted."[21]

Was his attitude to life going to be different now? Was it going to be different to women? In 1997 he told an interviewer he was finally coming around to the idea that he could live a traditional married life now, "in a nice little house with a lovely tablecloth and some nice crystal." He'd know how to treat a woman better than before, he said, and he'd enjoy having children. It wouldn't be like when he was with Elrod and had to slot himself into a mould in which he wasn't comfortable.

When the interviewer asked him if he had any concrete plans in this regard, however, he drew back. It made one wonder if he wasn't just playing with a new identity as he always played with identities, crafting new ones for each poem, each album, each concert. One learned to take remarks like this with many grains of salt from Cohen. As he wrote on the wall in Hydra all those years ago: "I change, I am the same, I change, I am the same."

Maybe all artists were chameleons who embraced antinomies. In *Beautiful Losers* he repeats the "I change, I am the same" epithet over an entire page. In "So Long, Marianne" he sings about laughing and crying simultaneously. In "Chelsea Hotel #2" he writes, "I need you, I don't need you."

He found it difficult to break the news to Roshi. In 1998 he wrote to him saying he wasn't able to "do" the monk lifestyle anymore. Beside the letter he enclosed a sketch of a nude, voluptuous woman. "Please forgive my selfishness," he wrote, signing the note, "Jikan, the useless monk."[22] He went on to call his publishing company Bad Monk.

Cohen visited India at the beginning of 1999 to study under the Hindu philosopher Ramesh Balsekar. He wasn't sure how long he was going to be there. It could, he said, be five minutes or five years. He was still searching for himself or for some version of himself that he'd failed to find in Mount Baldy. Was that person in love with life or meditation? With women or austerity? With performing or sequestering himself away from the masses? He never seemed to know, his priorities changing by the day.

As regards where he was going to go from here, it was anyone's guess. He still had his periods of depression. No hours of meditation could make these disappear. But he was better able to handle them now. Mount Baldy had given him that if nothing else. He threw out all the medication he was on at the end of that year, deciding that if he was to "go down," it was going to be with his eyes open.[23]

159

He claimed to be at peace with himself as the new millennium came in, saying he didn't have the cravings he'd had during the last one - cravings for success, for sex, even for companionship. "Time has purified me," he asserted. This was something coming from the "bad" monk.

Back on Boogie Street he entered pop culture in an unexpected way in 2001 when 'Hallelujah" was used in the Disney feature *Shrek*. In future years it would go on to become many people's favourite of all his songs. This, bizarrely, after being ignored when it first appeared on the B-side of *Various Positions* in 1985.

His return to the world of music, then, was serenaded by that endorsement of his value. It gave him the confidence to try and re-build his career. Whatever was wrong with him in 1993 had been sorted. Did he know how? No. He wasn't into those kinds of analyses. The bottom line was that he hadn't crashed and burned like Kurt Cobain or any of the other members of the 27 Club.

In many of the interviews he did at this time he said he was ready to re-connect with people on any level they wished now that he'd got rid of the "kink" that had been troubling him a few years before. Some of these are the most explicatory of his life. He ranges over the decades for fun like someone viewing himself from outside his own body. I experienced some of this myself in 1988.

 It's fascinating to listen to him expounding on everything he's asked, picking up on any nuance of a question to explore ways he might reply to it, going into every nook and cranny of his thought processes. Many other singers dealt in evasion tactics with interviewers, Bob Dylan being the most obvious example, but Cohen liked to engage with them on every level.

Many of his comments had an almost mathematical structure to them. Even when he spoke off the cuff it seemed somehow formal. He acted as if every question was a surprise to him even though one knew he'd been asked them hundreds of times before. He always tried to answer them differently, not only in the interests of giving a good interview but to keep his mind alive.

He did an interview on Scandinavian television in early 2001 where he talked frankly about his life with women. Asked why he never married he said it was probably due to the age in which he grew up, an age where people disputed the notion that they needed a piece of paper from church or state to ratify a union.

He raised some eyebrows when he said it was the woman rather than the man who was in charge of most relationships: "She decides within seconds of meeting a man whether or not she's going to give herself to him. I think in most cases the woman is running the show in these matters, and I'm happy to let them."[24]

No longer, however, was he the "ladies man" so he didn't have to concern himself too much about such matters. Asked in another interview what were the most important things for him now, he replied, "Health, work, and playing with the dogs."

His life became quiet after he left the monastery and that was the way he liked it. Anyone who visited his house would hardly have taken it for that of a famous singer. It was almost like an extension of his cabin in Mount Baldy - functional in the way of any suburban dweller. There were no fancy tables or chairs, no expensive paintings, no fluffy carpets.

He didn't go in for jacuzzis or penthouse suites. There wasn't a Maserati outside his door, just a Nissan Pathfinder. He'd had it for 25 years. Like himself (or a Volvo?) it kept going even when it had no right to. "I like to live simply," he stated. "That's not a virtue, it's just a preference. I like uncluttered spaces."[25]

He dressed in a low key manner too, despite having the reputation of being a clothes horse. Though he always looked elegant – "I was born in a suit," he joked - he didn't splurge out on designer suits. "Armani or your life" wouldn't have been a motto that sat well with him. By and large, he dressed off the peg.

Adam outlined some things people might not have known about his "downhome dad" when he said, "He loves George Jones and Hank Williams. He travels with one small suitcase. Many of his so-called "impeccable" suits are actually threadbare. He's only about five foot eight despite that giant baritone. He awakens at four in the morning and blackens pages every single day. He cuts his own hair. He's probably the best-known short order cook in the world."[26]

His next album was low key too, both in manner and matter. *Ten New Songs* was as undemonstrative a title as that of his first two - and, needless to say, *Recent Songs*. The content seemed to hark back to those days as well. Putting Sharon Robinson on the sleeve with him underlined the sense of humility. She played a huge part in its production. For years he'd wanted to acknowledge his debt to her. This seemed as good a way as any to do so.

It was partly recorded in her garage. She'd converted it into a studio. Cohen recorded separately in his own one. They collaborated both on the words and melodies and sang together on it.

His working relationship with her was simple. Both of them did what she called "the dirty" work" in private. Then they met to finesse it so that his words matched her vocals.

Robinson entered the partnership with Cohen almost without thinking. She felt comfortable with it right off. It was, she said, "like falling off a log."

He got up early to avoid having to worry about traffic interfering with the recordings. His favourite time of the day was from 4.30 a.m. to 9, when the phone started ringing. That was when his brain was most fertile. He also did some recordings after midnight - the best time, many people felt, to listen to Cohen.

As well as Robinson there was another woman involved, his treasured engineer Leanne Unger. Once again the comforting presence of women inspired him.

Ten New Songs was a different album to most of his recent ones, its "back to basics" sense a reminder to us of how he'd spent the past few years. The influence of Mount Baldy is everywhere on it. Cohen may not have brought the Ten Commandments down from the mountain with him like Moses but he brought ten incredible tracks.

When I bought this I installed a new sound system in my house to get the best out of it. When I played "In My Secret Life," the high-powered woofer had an incredible effect. It made the thumping music feel as if it was coming up through my feet. The pounding sound was even more effective on "That Don't Make It Junk."

Most of the tracks on *Ten New Songs* have a hypnotic effect. Maybe we could say that about all Cohen's work. Here it's particularly evident. "A Thousand Kisses Deep," "Love Itself," "Alexandra Leaving," he gives us all these gems like a case of reckless spending.

He liked the lyrics of "A Thousand Kisses Deep" so much he often recited it in a cappella fashion at concerts as if it was a poem. He dedicated it to a woman called Sandy Merriman who had cancer. She

163

found his music uplifting but the disease proved too much for her in the end. She took her own life in 1998.

The other numbers form a beguiling thread of yearning and rumination. There's humour and pensiveness in equal measure. Cohen leaves us guessing about the meaning of many of the songs, like "That Don't Make It Junk." Such ambiguity is apparent even from the oxymoronic first lines: "I fought against the bottle/But I had to do it drunk."

On the surface it seems to be a song about his abandonment of poetry for music ("I closed the book of longing/ And I do what I am told") but of course he never closed such a book. *The Book of Longing* would be published in 2006.

The album didn't fare too well in the U.S. but it was a hit in Europe. What else was new? A writer in *Rolling Stone* described it as Cohen's "most exquisite ode yet to the midnight hour."[27] That was due in no small part to his alluringly husky tone, the heritage, again, of those "50,000 cigarettes."

Cohen stopped smoking in 2002 after experiencing congestion in his lungs. He feared the worst so he went to his doctor. He put a camera up his nose. "Well," he asked him, "Do I have it?" – "it" being cancer. The doctor said he didn't yet but he was on the "royal road" to it. That was enough for him to give up the "coffin nails."

The new album got people talking – and writing – about him. His former Hydra neighbour Roger Green, an English teacher on the island, wrote a book called *Hydra and the Bananas of Leonard Cohen* in 2003.

It was a mythological journey through various themes. Adam felt the use of his name in the title was exploitative. Cohen didn't mind. He enjoyed Green's speculations about him and his life. At one stage of the book Green compares Suzanne Elrod to various literary and Biblical characters. Cohen admired his imaginative zeal.[28]

By now he was living with his Hawaiian girlfriend Anjani Thomas. He loved her voice. They discussed the possibility of her taking on some of his songs or putting his poetry to music. That would happen down the line.

He lived in the same house with Thomas but on a different floor. "I like to wake up alone," he explained.[29] Marianne was one of the few people in his life that this didn't apply to over a long stretch. It only applied to Elrod in the early stages of their relationship.

Thomas, like so many women before her, wanted Cohen to be her exclusive lover but that was never going to happen. His mercurial temperament warred against such an eventuality. He was generous to her with money but not with his time. Aviva Layton summed him up when she said, "If I needed $50,000, it would be there the next minute. But rely on him on a daily basis? You could not depend on that. [30] Very few people knew him as well as this lady.

Cohen has sometimes been accused of seeing women as sex objects. Whatever about her predecessors, this didn't apply to Thomas. Before her, he confessed, he often saw women from the perspective of his "urgent needs and desires." Mount Baldy - or age - changed that. He was now mature enough to view them as entities in their own right.

He brought out another album the following year. He was now seventy. *Dear Heather,* like *Ten New Songs,* was recorded both in his home and that of Sharon Robinson. Thomas also had a part in it. Leanne Ungar and Henry Lewy were involved in the production end. By now these people were like his private repertory company. At seventy maybe he needed such a comfort zone.

165

He originally wanted to call it *Old Ideas* but Columbia thought that made it sound like a compilation album. He "parked" the title but would use it for another album in a few years time.

He speaks some of the songs and sings others with Thomas and Robinson. One is aware of an eclectic feel to the album because of the ragbag of material. "On That Day" is a song about 9/11. "The Faith" is based on a Quebec folk song. There's a brilliant rendition of a country number, "Tennessee Waltz." This song is a barometer for singers, their ability to do it justice almost like a quantifier of their talent. We think of Tom Jones, Emmylou Harris, Tom Waits, even Elvis Presley. Elvis did a drunken version of it ("Tennessee Horse!") one night with the "Memphis Mafia" in Graceland when he wasn't even aware he was being recorded.

Dear Heather also includes some poems, most notably Lord Byron's "Go No More A-Roving." This was dedicated to Irving Layton, who was now suffering from dementia. Cohen includes a sketch of him on the sleeve notes. There are also sketches of some of the other people he serenades.

The album itself was dedicated to his publisher Jack McClelland. He'd died shortly before it came out. "Nightingale" is a poignantly written elegy to Carl Anderson. He'd also died that year after contracting leukaemia. Anderson was a friend of Cohen's. An actor, he'd played Judas in the film *Jesus Christ Superstar.*

"To a Teacher," a poem from Cohen's 1961 book *The Spice Box of Earth,* is here put to music and dedicated to A.M. Klein. Klein was a Montreal poet he'd known from his time in McGill University. He died in 1972. Cohen had great respect for his work. Sadly, he succumbed to mental illness in later years, resulting in him being incarcerated in what Cohen refers to here as "the silent loony bin."

Dear Heather was too diffuse to have a readymade listenership. It had great moments but no unifying thread. Cohen's best albums were the ones that came after a long gap, like *I'm Your Man* and *Ten New Songs*. Despite some deeply-felt sentiments and a sonorous sound, this one gives off a vibe of having been cobbled together from tracks that didn't fit on earlier ones. The disconsolate tone made it unappealing to listeners.

Cohen didn't make any effort to promote it. By now, people who liked him liked him and those who didn't, didn't. Maybe it had always been that way.

The Deal is Rotten

A man entered a boutique that Lorca owned in L.A. one day in 2005. He was dating an employee of Kelley Lynch. "Your father needs to check his accounts," he told her.

Lorca rang Cohen. He went to his bank. After a chat with the manager, he learned to his horror that most of his money was gone. Lynch had stolen over $10 million from him. She'd also forged documents and sold the rights to many of his songs.

Upon an initial exploration of one of his accounts he discovered she'd withdrawn $75,000 from it to pay off a credit card bill. He immediately revoked her signing powers. This was done just in time. In the same afternoon she tried to withdraw another $40,000 from the account.

When he got home he rang her to tell her the game was up. It wasn't a call he wanted to make. He'd never fired anyone before in his life. She answered cheerily. He lost no time in telling her that he was removing her name from anything to do with his accounts.

Lynch had been a friend of his for over two decades. Before he went into Mount Baldy he gave her power of attorney over his affairs. It even extended into the state of his health. She was delegated as the person who decided whether he was to be revived or not in the event of becoming unconscious. He trusted her with his life. "Kelley Lynch *is* Leonard Cohen," he said once.

He made the mistake of trusting her too much. In 1998 he told a reporter from *Billboard* magazine, "I've been making a living almost exclusively because of Kelley."[1]

"I went on holidays with her," he said, "with her children and my children. I thought she'd take a bullet for me." Famous last words.

He said to his friend Pico Iyer, "Somebody's next to you for eighteen years, your lover, friend, protector, guardian, voice in the world. Then suddenly this happens and you think: One of my closest friends in the world. Was I duped from the get-go?"[2] It made him question his judgment of people.

This was usually spot-on. It had been way off here. How could he have given so much power to someone, so much control over so much of his life? He'd hardly have given more to one of his children.

Iyer asked him how much was gone. He gave a dramatic answer. "I have hardly enough left to buy a cup of coffee," he informed him. This wasn't strictly speaking true. He had houses in Montreal, Hydra and Los Angeles.

Lynch hadn't touched these. She couldn't have. But he knew how serious things were. "I was fast approaching a situation," he said, "where I could put my card into an ATM machine and nothing would come out."[3]

The main problem was cash flow. Thirty years of earnings from his recordings and concerts had been wiped out. She'd also rifled his retirement money. And he owed a fortune to the tax man. How could someone spend that much money? He was informed that a lot of it went on holidays, on hotels, even meals.

As time went on he started to view the situation more objectively. Nobody had died. He still had a roof over his head. And he was still eating three square meals a day.

Another part of him felt numb. It was the same numbness he felt when Jeff Chase took the rights of "Suzanne" from him. That was when he was starting out. He could have been forgiven for a certain degree of naiveté then. But to be robbed at the age of 72? Fool me once, shame on you; fool me twice, shame on me.

Maybe, he thought, he shouldn't have been surprised. He'd never been the type to pore over his accounts. Lynch knew that. She also knew he wasn't the type who'd be looking to buy a yacht or a 16-room mansion.

He'd also gone into a monastery. Did she think he'd "lost it?" That he was so holy he wouldn't miss a few million?

He started to dig deeper into what she'd done with the money. There were some predictable purchases, like designer clothes, but also some weird ones, like gigolo expenses. Kelley Lynch employing a gigolo? Surely not.

She'd bought a condo for her parents. Nice. Then she set up a greeting card company – which flopped.

She bought her son a BMW car for $70,000 which he wrapped it around a tree. So she bought him another one. Well why not? Take two, they're small. Lennie won't mind, son, he'll just feel sorry for you.

Her high-flying corporate friend Betsy Superfon said Lynch accompanied her to places like Hawaii on vacations. She never knew where she was getting the money for such indulgences. Lynch told her she'd saved it. Superfon thought that must have been some kind of saving. When she quizzed her further she told her to do something physically impossible to herself. That was the way it was with Kelley. You were only allowed so many questions.

Superfon believed Lynch ripped Cohen off because she wanted a full blown love affair with him and he wasn't interested in giving her that. She saw the cheating as a "Hell hath no fury" thing.

He had a brief sexual relationship with her but never lived with her. ("I like to wake up alone." Lynch denied they were lovers, claiming he wanted to be and that she wasn't interested. She was good at turning truths back to front.

Lynch exhibited an inordinate degree of anger towards Cohen for reasons that aren't clear. Even the way she referred to him as "Cohen" instead of "Leonard" in all her comments about him shows that anger. Some of it could have been defensiveness, a Freudian slip resulting from her guilt over what she'd done to him.

She often made calls to him when she was drunk or under the influence of some other substance. The calls were abusive and sometimes sexual in content. She accused him of being a porn artist and a molester of Lorca. In other calls she threatened him.

He never spoke to her but he left his Ansaphone on, listening to them with growing incredulity. Many of the messages lasted ten minutes or more.

She also sent him emails at this time, some of them going on for up to fifty pages. He was getting twenty to thirty emails a day as well as the calls. On one call she said he needed to be "taken down and shot."[4] That comment stuck in his mind whenever he was on the street. Anytime a car slowed down, his heart missed a beat.

At a certain point, it's reasonable to assume, Lynch started believing her own lies. They were so outrageous there's no other explanation for them. Julie Eisenberg worked with her in the greeting card business. She said she enjoyed spreading zany rumours about Cohen, like putting the story about that he was pimping her out to his fellow monks in Mount Baldy.

Cohen knew Lynch was tough. That was one of the reasons he took her on. He felt he was too soft in business himself. That was the irony. She was now turning that toughness on him.

When the cat's away, as they say, the mice will play. Cohen was probably right to assume that once he put on his monastic robes, she saw her opportunity. It was what people called the Prospero Syndrome. He was, as it were, renouncing worldly goods. Ergo, she could play ducks and drakes with him.

Her streetwise ways, surprisingly, didn't extend to her covering her tracks very well. At times it seemed like she almost wanted to be found out. The things she spent the money on didn't always make sense. People who rob their bosses usually have more pragmatic outlets than gigolos.

And why did she spend it all? Was that not a surefire way of being found out? There's an old saying that goes, "When you're skinning a pig, leave enough skin for the next skinning." She didn't do that.

Lynch's 2006 extortions weren't her first overtures in this department. She'd already persuaded Cohen to sell the rights of his musical catalogue to Sony Music for $13 million. This was in two separate deals struck in 1997 and 2001. The reason she gave was that they weren't earning much in royalties. After going through his books, Cohen learned that this wasn't true, that the royalties were in the region of $4 million per year. He mainly agreed to the deals to save tax.

She put the Sony money into a company called Traditional Holdings, assuring Cohen that his children would be installed as its owners. This didn't happen. She took control of 99.5% of the company's assets, leaving only 0.5% for Adam and Lorca.

Traditional Holdings was overseen by an investment advisor called Neal Greenberg. He said he warned Cohen in emails that his funds were being depleted over the years and that he ignored such warnings. It's possible Lynch intercepted these emails and that he never saw them. Greenberg subsequently sued both Lynch (for extortion) and Cohen (for defamation).

Lynch had been married to a music producer called Steve Lindsey at the time of her first deal with Sony. She left him after he developed a problem with gambling. Lindsey felt she was in cahoots with Greenberg. Otherwise how could she have gained access to so much money?

Cohen dug further into his accounts, each revelation making him feel he was in a kind of black comedy featuring Sherlock Holmes as he followed the money trail. It went in so many directions, often he could hardly believe what he was seeing.

She bought 24-carat teeth chains for her children at $2000 a go. She spent up to $40,000 on purses. She played poker online for high stakes. And so on. Lindsey suspected she was haemorrhaging Cohen's funds for years but was nervous about being a whistleblower. He'd had a child with Lynch when they were married. They shared access. He was afraid she'd sue for full custody if he did anything to upset her.

Cohen was nervous about taking her on too. Lynch probably knew he would be. She once called him a wimp. He wasn't litigious, as he proved in 1977 when he refused to take Leo Sayer to court for his alleged plagiarism of "Famous Blue Raincoat." But if he didn't go to court this time he knew he'd be stuck with a massive tax bill. On money he hadn't even seen, never mind spent.

Cohen hated the pragmatic element of music. He went into the industry to make ends meet when his writing wasn't making him enough for him to live on. It had never been his priority but because of Lynch it had to be now.

Her actions caused a vast uprooting in his life. He was forced to shed his privacy in taking her to court. In ways it was similar to the way another recluse, Marlon Brando, had to revamp his lifestyle in 1994 when he too had to go to court. That was after his son Christian had been arrested for the second degree murder of his sister Cheyenne's fiancé Dag Drollett.

Cohen's path to court came about in a strange way. He was going through his accounts one day with Lorca and Anjani Thomas when Lorca (not Thomas, surprisingly) remembered that Thomas' former husband, Robert Kory, was a music industry lawyer. Would he be able to help? Cohen thought it was an avenue worth exploring.

He turned up at Kory's office one day with the classic line, "Hello. I may have lost a few million dollars."[5]

Kory had stopped practising law at this time but he went back to it for Cohen. He was happy to do so. He had, after all, grown up on his music. He said he'd work for him with his assistant, Michelle Rice.

Kory agreed to defer his fees until the matter was resolved, a gesture that touched Cohen deeply. This wasn't just unusual for L.A. lawyers, he said, it was unheard of. [6]

The first thing Kory did was organise a $1 million refund to Cohen from the IRS for taxes he'd already paid on the money he never saw. It was an important buffer to him to help him cope with his daily expenses – expenses he'd taken for granted for so many years - to his cost.

Official legal proceedings against Lynch began now. Cohen accused her of taking over $5 million from his retirement fund as well as significant other monies. The overall amount came to $9.5 million. She counter-sued him for defamation and (laughingly) extortion.

Lynch didn't fight him in court. This would have been pointless as she had no case against him. Instead she ran to her computer. The internet is often a haven for half-baked ideas and specious accusations.

One of her favourite ones was calling him a tax evader. Cohen countered, "Tax avoidance isn't the same thing as tax evasion."

Almost every utterance from her mouth in the years after he took her to court (and even before) was negative. As well as labelling him a tax cheat, she also called him a sex pest who delighted in hitting on women. The strings of abuse she unleashed seemed to be emanating from a deeply unhappy, deeply bitter woman.

She continued to deny any wrongdoing in the management of his affairs but in October 2005 Michelle Rice arrived at her door with a para-legal and two armed sheriffs in riot gear.

They ransacked her house and garage over the following two days, piling volumes of material onto a truck. Cohen was relieved to retrieve letters from people like Bob Dylan, Joni Mitchell and others which he feared had been lost.

Documents relating to the genesis of "Hallelujah" were also found. And, almost equally preciously, a drawing he'd done of a bird that went on to become the cover of *Book of Longing*.

There were thirty boxes of diaries, notebooks, sketches and personal documents in her house altogether. Cohen broke down in tears when he saw them. He knew she'd been flogging many of his effects on eBay and feared these "treasures" were among them.

A decision was given against Lynch at the end of that year. She lost her house as a result of this. To most people that would have been a shock but Lynch wasn't like most people. She appeared to be unperturbed about the ruling, departing the house with apparent nonchalance and taking to sleeping on a beach in Santa Monica. At times she resembled an ageing hippie.

Lynch was adjudged to owe Cohen over $7 million in all. She acted casual about this too. Pleading bankruptcy, she said she had no money to pay the amount.

She continued to make threatening phone calls to Cohen. By now he could only shake his head in bewilderment at them. He spent the next two years going through figures. God, he told a friend, must have wanted him to die of boredom.[7]

He hadn't been in a bank for years. How many had he entered since that day in London when he saw the suntanned cashier who told him about Hydra? He couldn't say.

In the following months he managed to get back a certain amount of the money Lynch misappropriated but not as much as he needed to live on. He was hoping to be awarded the proceeds of her house but she'd stopped paying the mortgage on it shortly after buying it so it was repossessed.

He had expenses to meet on a daily basis so he needed hard cash for these. Then there were the debts. And the tax bill. Where was he going to get the money to pay these?

He considered doing another album. Was that the best way to go? Even if it sold well, it would only cut a tiny way into his debts. He was informed he needed to tour. That was here the big money was.

Cohen had said to an interviewer in 1966, "I'm not interested in an insurance plan for my work." But that was now what his career seemed to be about now – expediency.

Where had his big dreams gone of being "as good as Bob Dylan?" What happened to three decades of singing, writing, touring? How could he be repaid for all the hours of crawling around hotel rooms in his underwear looking for a word that rhymed with "orange"?[8] If he decided to go back on the road - presuming people wanted him - he thought he'd be doing little more than, as he put it, singing for his supper.

A promoter called Rob Hallett came on board. He said he thought it would be a brilliant idea to tour. Cohen didn't agree at first. He protested, "I'm 73 years of age and I haven't played a guitar for ten years. What if it's a disaster?"

Hallett had been a fan of his since the early seventies. When his sister brought an album of his home one day he started listening to it and became hooked. Afterwards he got into his poetry.

He told Cohen he loved everything he'd written and sang during his long career. Cohen was touched by his devotion. Fans like this didn't come along every day of the week.

"There are lines you wrote," Hallett told him, "that helped me get where I am today."[9] His words melted Cohen. How could he refuse his request after such an accolade? He said he'd do the tour.

After they shook hands on the deal, Hallett started quoting lines of his poetry to him. Then he asked him if he could have a photograph taken of himself with him. It was the ultimate geek gesture. Maybe it was like my own geek gesture of showing Cohen my collection of short stories in 1988. (There was another comparison between Hallett and me too: A woman had gotten both of us in on him.)

After the initial euphoria of his decision to tour, Cohen repeated his concerns about not whether he'd have an audience anymore. Hallett said he believed he had. He further reassured him by telling him that if he changed his mind about touring after completing the rehearsals he wouldn't owe Hallett anything. Cohen said he hoped it wouldn't come to that.

A part of him was looking forward to "cobbling a little nest egg together again." He went home that night feeling good about himself for the first time in a year. Maybe, he thought, Hallett could undo the nightmare of Kelley Lynch. He fell asleep almost as soon as his head hit the pillow. That was something he hadn't been accustomed to recently.

When he woke up the next morning it was as if a new life was beginning for him. He stumbled out of bed and got ready for the struggle.

First We Take Fredericton

There's a school of thought that says God made Lynch defraud Cohen to get him back on the road again. Bankruptcy became a spur to him. He had to work so he did, digging down into his reserves of inspiration to re-awaken his muse. His financial woes ignited a desire for performing that he wasn't even aware he had anymore.

One of the epithets associated with touring is, "They don't pay you to sing, they pay you to travel." Another is, "Sometimes the sound checks take longer than the concerts." It was these peripheral areas around his comeback that gave him pause rather than the actual singing.

Going back to live performing was also going to involve a total revamp of his lifestyle. As Judy Collins jibed, "Leonard doesn't even go out of the house. How is he going to go out of the state?"

The last concerts he'd done had been in the early nineties. They'd been performed with the help of many bottles of wine. His liver was now too delicate for those kinds of indulgences. He'd have to go cold turkey.[1] That was going to be a challenge. He also worried about forgetting the words to his songs.

Hallett decided to ease him into things, setting up his first concert in a little-known Canadian town called Fredericton. A member of his crew joked, "First we take Fredericton, then we take Berlin."[2]

He told Barrie Wexler he was worried about what kind of numbers he'd draw. Wexler said, "They'll be hanging from the rafters." Cohen muttered, "That's probably what I'll get - a suicidal audience."[3]

People were indeed hanging from the rafters in Fredericton. There wasn't a spare seat in the venue. The concert could have been sold out ten times over. All those lonely souls who'd listened to Cohen in their bedsits in the seventies wanted to do so again now.

He was shaking as he stepped on stage on the first night. It was like when he appeared in his first concert with Judy Collins. But as soon as he stood in front of the audience, all his fears went away. He got a standing ovation.

He hadn't even sung a note at this point. Afterwards he was flying. He played for over three hours. Bigger shows followed. The more of a reaction he got, the more his confidence grew.

As well as the concerts, Kory organised the re-issue of some of his albums. There was also an exhibition of his drawings, a documentary film (*I'm Your Man*) and another book of poetry, *The Book of Longing*.

This had been so many years in the works, Cohen dubbed it the book of "Pro-Longing." Anjani Thomas also released her album *Blue Alert* at this time. It was all happening.

He turned up at a Toronto bookshop to launch both the book and the album. It was his first public appearance in over a decade. Over 3000 people attended the event.

Many streets surrounding the shop even had to be closed. The owner had earlier offered signed copies of the first 1500 orders to be placed online. They sold out within hours.

The songs on the album were co-written by Thomas and Cohen. He didn't sing on it but his voice could be "heard" through Thomas' delivery just as it could on Jennifer Warnes' *Famous Blue Raincoat* in 1987. His invisible guitar was her "secret chord."

Cohen didn't do any interviews during this stage of his comeback. That meant he was able to give his full attention to the shows. The fact that he wasn't smoking or drinking also helped.

If anyone was in any doubt that audiences came to see him out of pity over his financial circumstances, these were soon dispelled by the rapturous responses the concerts received. He'd never been this well received even in his heyday. "I can't walk out of my hotel to get a hot dog," he told Eric Lerner.[4]

Irving Layton died at the beginning of 2006. He was 93, a good age for a hellraiser. "Alzheimer's couldn't silence him," Cohen said at his funeral, "and neither will death." He praised him as being Canada's greatest poet and its greatest champion of poetry.

"Irving would have been very angry," he added, "if he knew there were this many people here and none of his poems were read." So he read a selection of them.

Back on the road he sang all the old hits, and some more recent ones, to ever-growing audiences. Only 700 people had attended the Fredericton concert. Less than two months later he was playing to 100,000.

"About three million dollars and sixteen shows in," Hallett crowed, "we knew we had a monster on our hands." The deal may have been rotten but it looked like old black Joe wasn't going to have to pick cotton for a while yet.

He'd been around so long he was like a relic. But he was still relevant to people's lives. "You write a song," he said, "and it slips into the world and they forget who wrote it. Then you hear it again 300 years later. Some women are washing their clothes in a stream and one of them is humming it." [5]

Audiences revered him like a prophet returning to prominence. There was a near-reverential silence at many of his concerts, particularly during the slow numbers.

181

He was described as being "the Sistine Chapel of live music."[6] Touring, he said, made him feel like being part of a motorcycle gang.[7] "I was sent," he declared, "like a postcard from one destination to another."[8]

He rang Sharon Robinson in 2008 to ask her if she'd like to go on the road with him. It had been almost thirty years since they'd sang together before. "I can't talk," she said, "I have laryngitis." Cohen said, "Can you sing?" He employed Hattie and Charley Webb as his backup singers as well. All three of them accompanied him in hundreds of concerts in the following years.

The Webb sisters had to go back to their native England to get visas before they could become fulltime band members. Once they did that, the "sublime" sisters, as he called them, established a rapport with him that he cherished.

Anytime they did a solo, most notably on the song "If It Be Your Will," he appeared to be entranced listening to them. Sometimes he tipped his hat to them, and to Robinson, appearing to almost "court" them in the view of one writer. [9]

He gave himself to his shows in the way Bruce Springsteen did. And as was the case with Springsteen, audiences showed their appreciation with generous reactions. Cohen sometimes seemed surprised by these. When people told him he was "the hottest ticket in town" he looked at them as if they had two heads.

Sometimes on stage he stopped singing to just look around him and savour the elation he felt. After the cheers died down, he acted as if he wasn't fully sure he'd really heard them.

There was no way he could have predicted this response when he talked with Robert Kory and Ken Hallett about the advisability of touring after a twelve year recess. How, he wondered, would Walter

Yetnikoff react to it all. Would he still hold the view that Cohen wasn't "any good"?

At a concert in London he spoke to the audience in a manner that doubled as a kind of mini- biography: "It's been a long time since I was on stage here. It was about fourteen or fifteen years ago. I was sixty years old - just a kid with a crazy dream. Since then I've taken a lot of Prozac, Pxel, Welbutrin, Effexor, Ritalin, Focalin. I've also studied deeply in the philosophies and the religions. But cheerfulness kept breaking through."

It was no doubt a speech that he rehearsed beforehand - most of his comments between songs on stage were - but who cared. The "cheerfulness" quip actually went back to the 17th century playwright Ben Jonson. The point was that the "high priest of heartache" had warmed his way back into people's hearts. No matter where he went, the red carpet was rolled out for him, the fans of yore rocking to his rhythms as if he'd never gone away.

German audiences he found to be particularly hospitable to him. This removed any feelings of hostility he may have harboured towards that country because of what Hitler had done to his predecessors.

Elvis Presley used to say, "The audience is the show." Cohen agreed. Audiences lifted him to new heights, enabling him to elevate songs he'd sung hundreds of times before into different places.

He may not have had the range of Sinatra but he carried his aura on stage, especially when he was wearing his fedora. There were actually rumours of Sinatra being interested in recording an album of his songs at one point but nothing came of it. (Cohen preferred Dean Martin).

183

He felt almost embarrassed at being the recipient of so much goodwill. Were there no young singers around who could fill stadiums better? At one of his concerts in 2008 he told the audience he was having a drink with Roshi one night when Roshi, who was then 102, said to him, "Excuse me for not dying." Cohen said he felt the same way now.

He became more theatrical as the concerts went on, feeding off the energy that came from the crowds. He often went down on one knee and cupped the microphone, turning his growl into a whisper as he invited the audience to partake of the unique intimacies of Cohenland.

His energy amazed people. Where did he get it from? "Love of what I do," he confided.

That was what sustained him through good times and bad. There was no other way he could have gone on as long as he could. He'd started late in music but was going on longer than most, his wingspan putting the young upstarts to shame. In ways he was like Bob Dylan with his "Never Ending" tour.

Cohen attended a Dylan concert in 2008. Dylan mainly kept his back to the audience during it. For part of the show he sat down. He was suffering from arthritis now. His renditions of his songs were so obscure, Cohen had trouble recognising some of them even when he was half way into them. None of this was unusual. Neither, in Cohen's view, did it matter greatly. He'd attained such a status in his field, he could set his own agenda. The loyal faithful were hardly likely to walk out.

Cohen met Dylan once in Canada. Dylan asked him how long it took him to write "Hallelujah." "Two years," he said. (It was actually four). He then asked Dylan how long It took him to write his song "I and I." Dylan replied, "About fifteen minutes." [10]

Nana Mouskouri saw the two of them together one day. "Neither is what you'd call a talker," she remarked, "o the conversation was like watching a game of chess." One imagines them circling one another like prize fighters, each admiring the other's genius but being a bit apprehensive about it as well, as if it could somehow pose a threat to them. Dylan once said Cohen was the only man he'd trade places with if he was offered the choice.

The main difference between the songs of Cohen and Dylan manifested itself mostly when they were singing about relationships between men and women. Dylan's "protest" style tended to extend to matters of the heart as well.

Cohen's love songs, even when he was writing of problems between couples, were generally gentle. Dylan has of course written gentle love songs to and about women but his tone tends to be more abrasive to them.

Even when Cohen was writing about the break-up of a relationship he tended to be more muted than Dylan. There's a big difference, for instance, between "So Long, Marianne" and "It's All Over Now, Baby Blue."

Both of their careers went on much longer than expected. Many people thought Cohen might have cut his wrists somewhere like the Chelsea Hotel before he reached forty, possibly while listening to one of his own songs. Dylan had survived despite having lived life in the fast lane for much of his life.

Each man had ingested his share of drugs. Not for nothing had Cohen been dubbed Captain Mandrax in his early years. As for Dylan, he was so bombed in many of his concerts he looked like he could have given Keith Richards a run for his money in the substance abuse department.

Both had survived. What did that say about their resilience? Probably that no matter how many parties they attended or how wasted they became at them in the early hours of the morning, they always had one eye fixed on their productivity, the next lyric or melody that might enhance their repertoire the following dawn.

Age was relative. Some singers were old at twenty. Some were even in their grave by that age. Cohen had been written off more times than most of us have had hot dinners.

His secret was an ability to roll with the punches, to accept the troughs that were part of the territory. As long as his mind was alive he knew more songs would come.

As we age, he told Larry Sloman, the brain cells associated with anxiety begin to die. "So despite our physical deterioration, it won't feel that bad." It seemed to apply to him. Sloman observed, "When others of his age could barely make it to their Early Bird dinners, he ended each show by skipping off the stage."

He didn't want to be young again. There was too much angst around. It reminded him of himself when he was that age. People debunked him for it then.

They weren't doing so now. Time had "allowed" him to be whatever kind of singer he wanted. He didn't have to apologise for the classical allusions in his songs, the Lorcan hermeneutics, the spiritual or quasi-spiritual spiritual imagery. They were all part of the package.

Jeff Buckley covered "Hallelujah" in 2008, going to number 2 in the UK charts with it. A version of the song recorded that year by Alexandra Burke topped the charts.

Cohen's own version entered the charts at number 34, thereby creating the unprecedented situation of the same song being in the top 40 three times by three different singers. It's a scenario that never took place before with any song and will hardly do so again.

Burke won *The X Factor* singing it. After being released as a single it sold over 100,000 copies in a day. By January 2009, UK sales of it passed the million mark.

Someone once described "Hallelujah" as "Hey Jude" for introverts. Maybe it would be more appropriate to call it "Hey Jude" for evangelists. The Irish musician Glen Hansard remarked, "Cohen made the word 'Hallelujah' hip." [11]

It wasn't the first time another singer had more success with one of his songs than he had. If Judy Collins made "Suzanne" suitable for public consumption, people like Burke and Buckley did likewise with "Hallelujah."

There were so many cover versions of it recorded over the years, Cohen eventually almost became embarrassed by them. The song threatened to overshadow all the other great ones he wrote. He experienced a mild sense of revenge at his record company for boycotting it upon its original release. but this was overkill. He eventually declared a moratorium on it.

Meanwhile the concerts went on. They were so successful, he found it hard to say no to any new dates that were put on his calendar. Was he in danger of burning himself out like he'd done in the early nineties?

There was always that possibility. He fainted on stage during a concert in Valencia on September 18, 2009. Food poisoning was later diagnosed. He was admitted to hospital. Three days later, on his 75th birthday, he did another concert in Barcelona. The message was clear. He was going to die with his boots on.

A video of the Isle of Wight concert he did at the beginning of his career came out that year. *Live At The Isle of Wight* finally reached the public nearly four decades after the concert it featured. The quality of the sound wasn't ideal but it was still grabbed up by fans who saw it as Cohen's "lost" concert.

The sleeve notes that came with it were interesting, giving brief histories of the songs he sang and the way he introduced them. Of "One of Us Cannot Be Wrong" we were informed, "This was written in a peeling room in the Chelsea Hotel when I was coming off amphetamines and pursuing a blonde lady that I met in a Nazi poster."[12] That was obviously Nico.

Earlier in the year Phil Spector was sentenced to nineteen years in jail after being convicted of the second-degree murder of Lana Clarkson, a friend and former lover of his. She'd been shot in the mouth with a handgun in his house in 2003.

Spector claimed she was depressed and shot herself. It would be very unusual for a person to commit suicide in someone else's house, especially by putting a gun in their mouth. And of course Spector had a history of being reckless with guns, right back to the recording sessions with Cohen.

The evidence on which he was convicted was conclusive. His DNA was all over Clarkson. There were even powder marks from the bullet that killed her on his clothing. Before she joined Spector that evening she'd been filling in her tax returns. It was hardly the behaviour of a suicidal person. Spector showed no remorse for what he did.

Cohen was visited by the FBI after his arrest. The story of him putting a gun to Cohen's head when they were recording *Death of a Ladies Man* was well known.

The detectives thought Cohen might have had more stories of Spector's propensity towards violence but he hadn't. He told them it was an isolated incident and that he wasn't willing to propose it as anything relating to what happened to Clarkson. As a result of this he wasn't consulted again.

In 2009, documentary film-maker Tony Palmer discovered nearly 300 rolls of film he thought had been lost from his 1972 documentary *Bird on a Wire*. This meant he could now re-cut it to his (and Cohen's) satisfaction.

He released it the following year, receiving permission from Pablo Picasso's estate to feature his "dove of peace" on the cover. The film at last received the attention it should have 36 years before, winning the Grierson Award for Best documentary in 2011 and a Gold Medal at the New York film and TV Festival the following year.

Cohen still kept singing. Many of the concerts took place in Dublin. I went to them when I could and was always glad I did so. The atmosphere was usually electric. It was so different from the National Stadium in 1988.

He was now in a different venue, the Point Depot. It was as large as a Roman amphitheatre and he filled it. I remembered the quiet man who'd spoken to me in that small room in Jury's Hotel. He still looked quiet but there was a different kind of aura about him now than there had been on that rain-soaked night. As he poured out his melodies he was like a guru chanting mantras from the top of Mount Baldy.

He was originally only supposed to do one night on his first visit to Dublin but the tickets sold out in a half hour so two more were added.

Bono asked to see him after the first one but he said he was too tired. The U2 frontman then asked him if he'd like to have lunch at his house the following day.

Again Cohen demurred. When Bono asked if he could meet Cohen after the second show and Cohen gave him a third snub, he backed off. It was a very surprising turn of events. Everyone knew how much Bono admired him. Maybe age was catching up on him. Whatever the reason, Bono accepted it.

He did two open air shows in Yeats' Lissadell in County Sligo in 2010. This was sacred ground to him. I tried to get tickets but they were sold out in milli-seconds. So was all the accommodation for miles around.

I didn't mind missing Sligo as much as I would have hearing him in an enclosed auditorium. I felt he needed that more than a Bruce Springsteen or a Neil Diamond.

It was the sense of intimacy, even claustrophobia, that always made his songs come alive for me.

To reiterate the old cliche, you felt he was singing to you and you alone in these venues. In the open air, I thought, the sounds sometimes seemed to disappear into the ether.

The concerts in Lissadell were among his favourites of all. He ran down the stairs after the first one, saying to the promoter John Reynolds, "That was magic. I can't wait for tomorrow."[13] It rained, perhaps inevitably for Ireland, but people danced in it.

Cohen was his usual humble self in Ireland. One day he appeared in the coffee shop the crew used. He joined the queue for breakfast without pulling rank. A piece of paper was stuffed under his nose by somebody who didn't know who he was. It had the words "Who are you working for?" on it. Cohen wrote, "Myself."

Before he left Sligo, Reynolds presented him with a book of Yeats' poetry signed by the poet himself. It became one of his most treasured possessions.

Lorca had a baby with the gay singer Rufus Wainright, a friend and fan of Cohen's, in 2011. "I'm off the evolutionary hook," he crowed, "I've done my bit." Wainright's partner Jorn Weisbrodt was listed as the "deputy father." The baby, a girl, was called Viva Katherine Cohen. Leonard was a very proud grandfather.

He became even prouder when he won the prestigious Prince of Asturias Award for literature later that year. Asturias was a principality in the North of Spain.

Each year the prince bestowed the award on an individual who was adjudged to have made a notable achievement in their field during the year. Cohen gave a powerful speech at the presentation, acknowledging the great debt he owed to Spain for inspiring his flamenco guitar technique.

He came back to Dublin again in 2012 to do a set of concerts in the grounds of Dublin's Royal Hospital in Kilmainham. This time I was luckier in booking tickets for myself and Mary. Cohen sang as beautifully as ever.

His voice sounded a little croakier than it had been when he was in the National Stadium or "The Point" (or 3Arena as it's now called) but it was no less impressive on that account. Maybe the croakiness even added to the emotion of the songs, intensifying the "broken heart" feeling they conveyed.

His audiences at these concerts comprised every facet of society - priests, politicians, beatnik poets, sensitive secretaries. Some of them were people I recognised from the time he was in the National Stadium when we were all young – or almost young.

Others were the new fans, the X Generation, people who'd been introduced to his music by their parents, their uncles or aunts, anyone who had a record player. They wandered up and down corridors gazing at me as if they knew me. And maybe they did, from what we all shared. They had a look of lostness in their eyes. Many of them seemed to have suffered or were still suffering.

Others seemed to have come through it. Had he guided them? Was he still doing so? This wasn't music as much as catharsis, the empathy of fellow strugglers in the battleground of life. "I never felt like I was God," he'd said to me that day in Jury's Hotel. But at times it seemed like he was.

He did a record dozen shows in Ireland between 2008 and 2013. I went to at least one of them on each occasion except for the time in Sligo.

I went to Dylan every time he came to Dublin too, even though some of his concerts were abysmal. Others were electrifying. I couldn't take the chance I'd miss one of the latter.

Dylan often said he liked to do his songs a different way every time he sang them as otherwise he got bored. Cohen was more predictable. That gave his audiences a sense of security. Could one have too much security? The problem with Dylan was that you never knew what you were going to get with him. The problem with Cohen, for some people, was that you did.

During these golden years between 2008 and 2013 he outstripped Dylan for me. He sold more tickets to his concerts in his seventies than in any decade before that. What other singer could claim such an achievement?

Cohen came to love touring in the last decade of his life. Why wouldn't he? Adulation is like oxygen to a singer and there was never any shortage of that. There was no uncertainty anymore, like in his early years where he didn't know what kind of reception he was going to get. The ageing troubadour was now preaching to the choir. "I love being on the road," he told his friends, "It's when I'm off it I get worried."

He was always aware that his gift paled in comparison to the "real" problems going on around him. One day he said to a reporter, "We're in a world where there's famine and hunger and people are dodging bullets and having their nails pulled out in dungeons so it's very hard for me to place any high value on the work I do." At the end of the day, singing was a job. More important things were going on outside it.

One of the things going on outside it for him now was the culmination of the Kelley Lynch case. There was no describing his relief when it ended.

Lynch was convicted not on the fraud charges, strangely enough, but for her harassment of him, and sentenced to 18 months in prison. Greenberg had already been charged with fraud by this time and fined heavily. Many people saw it as a pyrrhic victory for Cohen. Only a fraction of his money had been recovered.

Lynch had opted for trial by jury. Cohen sardonically thanked her for this, pointing out that it allowed the public to witness "her massive depletion of my retirement savings and yearly earnings." It gave him no pleasure to see his one time friend shackled to a chair. He said he hoped her incarceration would lead to a reform in her heart "from hatred to remorse."[14]

He did another album now. *Old Ideas* was a combination of jazz, blues and country and western. It was a curious mix, though Hank Williams had once called country music "Blues for white people." Cohen said he did it from a wish to get back to his roots. The lyrics, however, testify to a different kind of person than the impressionable debutante of yore. He's now "a lazy bastard living in a suit."

Old Ideas, as Chris Wade wrote in his insightful book *The Music of Leonard Cohen,* had an old man grappling with a young man's problems.[15] Maybe we could say that about all his later albums.

His age changed but his themes didn't. "I felt like Ronald Reagan," he said, "In his declining years he remembered he had a good role once. He'd played the part of a president in a movie. I kind of felt that somewhere I'd been a singer."[16]

Where would his next adventure come from? "Maybe I'll do a gig at some downscale casino in Vegas," he suggested to Eric Lerner, "I could be the Wayne Newton of the introspective gambling set,"[17]

By now he was coming to the end of his concerts. He'd done over 400 of them altogether.

The final Dublin ones were in 2012. There was an element of celebration at them but also poignance. "I hope to be back this way again soon, friends," he said at the end of the last one, tipping his fedora to us. I felt a lump in my throat as I listened to his words as I doubted he would. He was suddenly looking very frail.

He organised front row seats for Marianne at a concert he gave in Oslo the following year but he didn't meet her, getting caught up talking to a group that included Israel's ambassador to Norway.

She didn't impose herself on him; it wasn't her style. Always the lady, she cheered excitedly after he sang *"So Long, Marianne."* There were no leftovers of the relationship for her even yet. Both of them had gotten on with their lives without recrimination. That was how he could keep singing the song without any sense of her feeling rejected by it.

In some ways Cohen was like Ernest Hemingway. His first lengthy relationship with a woman, like Hemingway's with Hadley Richardson, was his purest, but he left her for more worldly ones. Both women married more grounded men afterwards but they forgave their first (more famous) lovers and kept up friendships with them for the rest of their lives, albeit from a distance.

Marianne wasn't Janis Joplin and "So Long, Marianne" wasn't "Chelsea Hotel#2."

The song was a tribute to her rather than a valediction.

Closing Time

F. Scott Fitzgerald once said there were no second acts in American lives. Cohen disproved that. His second act was his best one. It was the third he worried about, or at least the last part of it.

In 2013 he developed a rare blood disorder, ITP. His friend Robert Faggen gasped, "That's incurable." Cohen said calmly, "We all have to go some way." It eventually developed into leukaemia. Again he was philosophical about it. It was the way he'd been all his life, both with triumph and disaster. Nobody beat the rap.

For now, life went on. Sharon Robinson brought out a book of photographs that year called *On Tour With Leonard Cohen*. I was disappointed to find no text in this apart from an introduction by Larry "Ratso" Sloman, a longtime friend. The photos may not have won any prizes for inspiration but they provided an important guide to what it must have been like being on the road with him.

Robinson captured the ordinary moments press people weren't privy to, the behind-the-scenes goings-on of a group of people who obviously enjoyed being together hugely. We saw Cohen in his hotel room, at lunch, at airports, in cafeterias. There was even a shot of him putting some coins into a washing machine in a laundermat. Robinson tabulated all these events on her iPhone. Cohen credited her with having "an eye as fine as her ear." The book is hardly a classic collection in the way that, say, Alfred Wertheimer's book on Elvis Presley from 1956 is but it's an affectionate compilation all the same.

Roshi passed away later that year. He was 107. He wouldn't have to apologise to Cohen for "not dying" any more. After his death a series of revelations suggested that he'd been molesting, and possibly even raping, different women throughout his life. It's unclear if Cohen believed he was guilty of such crimes. He was aware of the allegations, and said in an interview a month before Roshi died that he was "a very naughty guy" but he didn't elaborate. [1]

Cohen turned eighty that year. "In my family we have a very charitable approach to birthdays," he chirped, "We ignore them." He said he planned to celebrate the start of his ninth decade by taking up cigarettes again. He thought it might improve his voice.

Brigitte Bardot sent him a birthday card. It was over forty years since he met Janis Joplin while searching for her in the Chelsea Hotel. "We're twins," she wrote on the card. She'd been born a mere week after him.

He released another album the day after his birthday. *Popular Problems* was his thirteenth studio album. It was a mixture of blues, gospel, country and soul. As was the case with *Dear Heather*, he also put two of his poems ("Nevermind" and "A Street") to music on it. The practice of recording in his house continued here. He co-produced it with Patrick Leonard, who co-wrote some of the songs with him. Cohen had also worked with Leonard on *Old Ideas*.

The first song on it was called "Slow." It was a sexually suggestive number that hardly applied to the speed at which the album was put together – or indeed the pace of the song itself. Did he feel he was running out of time and had to make the most of what he had left? Perhaps, but once again the intimations of mortality are more than compensated by his cheery tone. The album's sleeve had him scowling and carrying a cane but elsewhere his bittersweet humour is in evidence. He laughs through his tears as ever.

The critics and public alike loved *Popular Problems*. It was a success both in Europe and the U.S. That was a precedent for him.

Had it taken this long to take off on both continents simultaneously? There was life in the old dog yet. He said he was contemplating a sequel to it called *Unpopular Solutions*. By now his penchant for having us on had almost become a habit.

His mood darkened in subsequent months as events in the outside world tumbled in on top of him. His sister Esther died two months after Roshi. Then his friend Steve Senfield passed away. His own health had now gotten worse as well. "I'm in the departure lounge of life," he said. He didn't mind dying, he assured people, it was the "preliminaries" that were worrying. (That was an old Irving Layton line).

He told Christophe Lepold, who wrote a biography of him entitled *The Man Who Saw the Angels Fall* (thereby referencing his quote about Charles Bukowski), "Body insisting on gravitational rights."

Death was the ultimate fall. Osteoporosis had caused his spine to collapse. He was in a lot of pain but he didn't complain. All he asked was to be left alone when it was at its worst.

The Zen part of him accepted the fact that life was a rollercoaster with peaks and valleys. He'd been on a peak for a long time now. "Maybe God forgot about me for a while," he joked to Eric Lerner, "He was too busy torturing some other saps." Then someone must have tipped him off: "Psst. Check out Cohen over there. He's having a ball." [2]

No matter how bad he felt, he wanted to keep working. The prospect of death, as they say, concentrates the mind. In 2015 he brought out *Can't Forget,* an album of outtakes from his *Old Ideas* tour. It contained two previously unheard tracks, "Got a Little Secret" and "Never Gave Nobody Trouble," and also two covers, "La Manic" by the Quebec composer Georges Dor, which he sang in French, and

George Jones' "Choices." He'd finally gotten around to doing a number by his old c&w friend. A fine job he made of it too.

When he was sixty, an interviewer had asked him if he had any long-term plans. He said he'd once gone to a concert performed by the singer Alberta Hunter. She was 82 at the time. He felt blessed to be in her presence. Now he was approaching that age himself. So that was the plan – to be another Alberta Hunter.

What do you do when you're about to die? Make another album, of course. It was a no-brainer.

He called his swansong *You Want it Darker*. Adam produced it. Lorca was also with him most of the time now too. He wasn't mobile at this point so he had to sing from a chair, an adjustable mobile one. He recorded it on a work station he placed on his laptop. Some of the songs he dictated into his phone. "I'm trying to forget how fucked up the old vehicle is," he huffed. The old vehicle was his body. Even Volvos had to pack up sometime.

He had to be up before the birds started singing, before the drone of the traffic, before Lorca's dogs started barking. That wasn't usually a problem. He'd always been a dawn riser.

He didn't think he'd be able to finish the album at first. Then something happened. He felt himself being carried along by "a mysterious wind, and the grace of the occasion."[3]

The title had perhaps a little anger in it. All through his career he'd been castigated for being dark. Now he was throwing the term back at his listeners. It was as if it was our fault. We wanted it so he was giving it to us. It was the self-prophetic fallacy. The chickens had come home to roost.

His voice sounded deeper than ever on the album. One commentator said every word sounded like it was lifted off stone tablets.[4]

He had mixed feelings about Adam being its producer despite the fact that he got on so well with him. He liked his humility, saying that after Phil Spector he never wanted to work with an egoist again. but he didn't welcome the "family business" overtones of their collaboration. He'd baulked against that in his own life when it was suggested he become a tailor.

Some days he felt he couldn't sing. The words wouldn't come out. But he persevered. He said it was going to be the most important album of his life.

His Zen dharma friend David Rodin wondered why he was putting so much effort into it when he had hardly any energy left.

Cohen told him it was because of all the people who'd listened to him over the years. He wanted to thank them. This was his last chance to do so.

Like *Popular Problems*, it proved to be a great success. He lived long enough to witness this. It gave him the impetus to entrust Adam with the production of another one, *Thanks for The Dance*. This featured unused outtakes from *You Want It Darker* as well as other material. His voice was surprisingly strong on these songs. Adam believed this was due to his familiarity with the material: "He knew where the beat fell, where the syllables fell within that beat."

Even though he was in agony, the old pro was still hitting the marks. "Many of the vocals were first takes," Adam revealed, "They were birthed almost complete. A very rare thing." His body might have been betraying him but his voice wasn't.

Bob Dylan was aware of the failing health of his sometime friend. He said he loved *You Want It Darker* as much as anything Cohen had ever done in his long career. Dylan had just won the Nobel Prize. It was the first time the award had been given to a songwriter.

Cohen returned the compliment, saying he was delighted Dylan had received such an honour. He compared the bestowing of it to "pinning a medal on Mount Everest for being the highest mountain."

Some people thought Cohen should have been given the prize instead of Dylan. They felt it was a decision based on the fact that Dylan had made more money for the music industry than Cohen. This was a myopic view. Dylan did much more than that. Maybe it was time to stop comparing the two singers. One commentator said, "Leonard is for the heart and Dylan for the head."[5] That was about the size of it.

Cohen started to look back on his life, on all the great moments and the not so great ones. He'd given as much as he could to his music and to everything else – his children, his friends, the women he'd loved. One of the latter was now in as bad a health situation as he was.

In July of that year, a friend of Marianne wrote to Cohen to say she was dying of leukaemia. The news brought tears to his eyes. He wrote back, "Dearest Marianne, I'm just a little behind you, close enough to take your hand. This old body has given up just as yours has. I've never forgotten your love or your beauty. Safe travels, old friend. See you down the road." His reply went viral on social media. His words were so touching, so succinct: "Close enough to take your hand." Was he thinking of the handholding phrase from "So Long, Marianne"?

201

His message was read out to her as she lay in a hospital bed. She was in a lot of pain but she could still smile as she listened to it. "That was very beautiful," she said to the nurse who was attending her.

Cohen stopped giving interviews in his last months. After six decades of answering the same questions there was nothing more to be said. He made his last public appearance at a press reception in Los Angeles on October 13.

He was as thin as a rake and apparently in pain but he still gave a speech. He didn't make any plea for sympathy but everyone knew what he must have been going through. It was even apparent in his voice, in the slow way he spoke, in how he paused uncharacteristically between sentences. He was as gracious as ever but the life seemed to have gone out of him. It was as if he was saying goodbye to the world without using the word.

Later that month he spent a week in the Cedar-Sinai hospital, ostensibly to have his "plumbing" fixed. At home he was too tired to meet people. He communicated with them through emails instead. His medication helped the pain he was going through but not all the time. To alleviate it he had cement injected into his vertebrae. Many of them were fractured.

He became bad-tempered on occasion, something that was so out of character for him. It was usually when the effects of his medication weren't kicking in. He gave out to Lorca one day when he thought she was rude to Paul Muldoon, an Irish poet he'd become friendly with. Another time he became annoyed with an interviewer who got the time of a proposed interview wrong. When she finally arrived he was in too much pain to talk to her.

He asked a rabbi, Mordecai Finley, if his soul would survive death. Finley assured him it would be around for a long time. "I'm ready to die," he told friends, "I hope it's not too uncomfortable." That was as much *angst* as the so-called "prophet of doom" exhibited. He put his affairs in order, right down to details like giving his car to the man who did odd jobs for him around his house.

The surprise wasn't that he was dying. It was that he'd lived so long. He'd outlasted those singers like Janis Joplin, Jimi Hendrix, Jim Morrison, Bryan Jones and all the others who died at 27, that so-called mandatory age for self-destructive rockers, by well over half a century. Kurt Cobain was the last "27-er" to "live fast, die young and make a good-looking corpse."

As he neared death, Elrod said she forgave him for all the problems between them. He was amused by this, thinking it was he that should have been forgiving her.

He had a fall on November 6 but refused to go to hospital. He had an internal haemorrhage afterwards. Then he slipped into a coma. He died the following day. "He didn't die because he fell," Aviva Layton pointed out, "He fell because he was dying."

He died by slow decay rather than in the merry merry month of May. Neither was he sure who was calling.

He'd only outlived Marianne by three months. They even died from the same disease. It was the final link in their unique chain of love. Their steps would always rhyme.

He was buried in an unadorned grave next to his parents. News of his death wasn't announced for three days to avoid a media circus. When it was, fans gathered round his house to hold a vigil. His passing led to a huge upsurge in sales of his records worldwide. *You Want It Darker"* went on to top the charts in thirteen countries.

203

Donald Trump was elected president of America the day afterwards. It seemed somehow appropriate. Beauty was going from the world and ugliness coming in.

Judy Collins thought the fact that his last album was called *You Want it Darker* seemed like an ironic prefiguring of the Trump victory. Cohen had actually predicted this, nay welcomed it. One had to confront the beast, he believed, before one could conquer it. He knew fundamentalism was on the rampage. Trump was merely the standard-bearer for an already existing malaise. Democracy was no longer coming to the U.S.A.

After people had digested the news that he was gone they started to assess what his contribution to the world of music had been. Most agreed that his main talent was for transporting one into an almost sacred space. He brought you into his world for the duration of a song, a concert, an album. You sat listening to him almost afraid to move as his plaintive strains washed over you.

Cohen inherited from Lorca the surreal imagery that infused his poetry and songs. From his ill-fated guitar teacher, despite the brevity of their encounter, he got the love of flamenco. Such words and music might not have gone anywhere were it not for the era in which he flourished. Despite being too old to be a folk singer and too young - and middle class - to be a Beat, he captivated an era.

His career was one of the unlikeliest in history. It basically emanated from his versatility. When his novels and poetry weren't selling, he turned sideways. How could a person be a best-selling poet and then just suddenly just "decide" to become a singer? His friend Ken Norris said, "Whatever he did, he would have been famous at. If he'd stayed in the clothing business there'd be a line of suits we'd all be wearing."

He was never precious about his ideas, varying his perspective depending on whoever he was with. He could discuss everything from Scientology to Est to the best place to get a beef sandwich. He merged the sacred and the profane, the holy and the broken, the old guard and the new disaffected.

Rebecca De Mornay was very saddened to hear of his death. "Losing him is like losing a limb," she remarked, "He faced death like he faced life, with honesty, grace and a breathtaking depth of perception."[6]

John Lissauer commended his dedication: "He was never on stage for less than two hours and forty-five minutes. He never phoned it in."

Maybe his Zen friend David Radin described him best of all when he said, "He was probably the most extraordinary and the most ordinary person I ever met."[7]

Aftermath

"You'll be hearing from me baby, long after I'm gone."

Tower of Song

Cohen's reputation has grown in the years since he died. There are an innumerable number of websites devoted to him. Books also continue to be written about the man and his music.

Many of them hark back to his relationship with Marianne, the love of his life. In 2017, an auction of more than fifty letters he wrote to her was held in Christies. They fetched almost $1 million.

Two years later a DVD was released called *Marianne & Leonard: Words of Love*.

It was directed by Nick Broomfield. He'd had a brief affair with her in 1968. It captured their relationship movingly with the help of unseen footage and many interviews conducted with those who knew them.

Broomfield was only 20 when he met her. He was on a cruise with his father at the time. She was 33 but the age gap wasn't a problem for either of them.

She played Cohen's music and read his poetry to him. As a former boarder at a Quaker school, he was profoundly ignorant of both at the time. They embarked on an affair and continued it in Cardiff, where he lived, after he left Hydra.

Hydra is now the playground of the rich. Gone is the spartan simplicity of the early sixties, a simplicity that was first compromised by that famous bird on the wire and has now innumerably more birds, more wires, more creature comforts and more blandness.

It's difficult to imagine anybody writing songs there now, or poetry, but the ghosts of Cohen and Marianne still haunt it, even in folk memory. The street on which they lived is now called Odos Leonard Cohen.

There have been problems with Cohen's estate since he died. In 2022, Adam and Lorca made arrangements to have Robert Kory removed from its management.

Everyone was shocked. They accused him of various misdemeanours, some of them surrounding *The Ballet of Lepers,* his abandoned novel from the 1950s which had now finally been published.

On September 21, 2024, what would have been Cohen's 90th birthday, I attended a concert in his memory in Dublin's 3Arena. Various performers sang his songs well.

We all felt bathed in the comfort they exuded. But there was something missing. The man himself. His image appeared on a large screen behind the performers from time to time but it only served to remind us of the fact that he wasn't there in the flesh.

One of the most moving songs sung that night was "Bird on the Wire." As I listened to it I thought of Kris Kristofferson's wish to have the first two lines of it put on his grave. A week to the day later, Kristofferson died. All the oaks were falling.

Kristofferson used to say he was able to drink a bottle of whiskey a day and still live as long as he did "because God loves poets and drunkards." Maybe he also loved poets and epicures like Cohen.

Will we ever see a performer like him again in the future?

It's hard to say. The era that spawned him is gone, having been replaced by one of synthesisers and canned music. Neither is the sensibility he highlighted particularly relevant to our time.

As one writer put it, "You'll never get another Leonard Cohen. Nobody wants to be Shakespeare now. They want to be the new Steve Jobs."

Notes

Born Like This

1. Liel Leibovitz, *A Broken Hallelujah*, 35.
2. Robert Dimery, ed., *Leonard Cohen In His Own Words*, 66.
3. Jim Devlin, *In Every Style of Passion*, 14.
4. Anthony Reynolds, *Leonard Cohen: A Remarkable Life*, 9.
5. Mike Evans, *Leonard Cohen: An Illustrated Record*, 10.
6. George A. Walker, *A Woodcut Biography*, 30.
7. *Marianne and Leonard: Words of Love*.
8. Niema Ash, *Nomad Girl*, 158.
9. Devlin, *In Every Style of Passion*, 14.
10. Evans, *An Illustrated Record*, 13.
11. Leonard Cohen Papers, December 11, 1963.
12. *Classic Interviews*.
13. Dennis O'Driscoll, ed., *The Bloodaxe Book of Poetry Quotations*, 14.
14. Tim Footman, Hallelujah, 16.
15. Ira B. Nadel, *Various Positions: A Life of Leonard Cohen*, 56.
16. *Saturday Night*, June 1969.

Came So Far For Beauty

1. Dimery, ed., *Leonard Cohen In His Own Words*, 13.
2. *Sunday Independent*, August 11, 2019.
3. Leibovitz, *A Broken Hallelujah*, 88.
4. Julian Cox and Jim Sheddon, eds., *Leonard Cohen: Inside His Archive*, 29.
5. Leibovitz, *A Broken Hallelujah*, 87 8.
6. *Marianne and Leonard: Words of Love*.

7. Tamar Hodes, *The Water and the Wine*, 26.
8. Letter from Cohen to McClelland, April 18, 1961, University of Texas.
9. Nadel, *Various Positions*, 91.
10. Harvey Kubernick, *Everybody Knows*, 33.
11. Cox and Sheddon, eds., *Inside His Archive*, 30.
12. *Ibid.*, 71.
13. *Village Voice*, No. 2, 2004.
14. Karl Hesthamer, *So Long Marianne*, 115.
15. *Song Talk*, April 1993.
16. *Village Voice*, December 28, 1967.
17. *Take 30*, May 23, 1966.
18. Hodes, *The Water and the Wine*, 107.
19. Judy Scott, *Leonard, Marianne and Me*, 79.
20. Letter from LC to Masha, March 10 1962, University of Texas.
21. Letter from LC to Masha, May 20, 1962.
22. *Ibid.*
23. Reynolds, *A Remarkable Life*, 225.
24. Letter from LC to Jack McClelland, December 18, 1961, University of Toronto.
25. Sylvie Simmons, *I'm Your Man*, 116.
26. David Boucher and Lucy Boucher, *Deaths and Entrances*, 110.
27. Nadel, *Various Positions*, 137.
28. *Village Voice*, December 28, 1967.
29. *Ibid.*
30. Michael Gnarovski, ed., *Leonard Cohen: The Artist and His Critics*, 165.
31. Michael Posner, *That's How the Light Gets In*, 441.
32. *Saturday Night*, June 1969.

33. *Marianne and Leonard: Words of Love.*
34. Evans, *An Illustrated Record*, 36.

From Page to Stage
1. Kubernick, *Everybody Knows*, 68.
2. Evans, *An Illustrated Record*, 21.
3. *Classic Interviews.*
4. *McGill Reporter*, January 20, 1967.
5. Alan Light, *The Holy or the Broken*, 1.
6. Michael Fournier and Ken Norris, eds, *Take This Waltz*, 140.
7. *Ibid.*, 25.
8. Andy Warhol and Pat Hackett, *POPism*, 261.
9. Paul Barrera, *Came So Far for Love: The Words and Music of Leonard Cohen*, 11.
10. Leibovitz, *A Broken Hallelujah*, 10.
11. Walker, *A Woodcut Biography*, 78.
12. *Guardian*, January 19, 2012.
13. Nadel, *Various Positions*, 245.
14. Judy Collins, *Sweet Judy Blue Eyes,* 200.
15. Kubernick, *Everybody Knows*, 42.
16. Judy Collins, *Trust Your Heart: An Autobiography*, 147.
17. Michael Posner, *The Early Years*, 355.
18. Hesthamer, *So Long Marianne*, 182-3.
19. Kubernick, *Everybody Knows*, 34.
20. Karen O'Brien, *Joni Mitchell: Shadows and Light*, 68.
21. *Ibid.*, 293.

So Long, Marianne
1. *I'm Your Man*, Lian Lunson DVD.
2. John MacKenna, *Absent Friend*, 45.
3. Simmons, *I'm Your Man*, 174.
4. Posner, *The Early Years*, 434-5.
5. *Time*, October 13, 2001.
6. *Hallelujah: A Journey, A Song*.
7. *Mojo*, January 2012.
8. *CBS Music*, November 11, 2016.
9. Jeff Burger, *Leonard Cohen on Leonard Cohen*, 243.
10. BBC Radio 4, June 1998.
11. Jason Holt, ed., *Leonard Cohen and Philosophy*, 110.
12. *Mojo*, January 2012.
13. *Ibid.*
14. Kubernick, *Everybody Knows*, 144.
15. *Song Talk*, April 1993.
16. Hesthamer, *So Long Marianne*, 169.

Famous Blue Leonard
1. *Elm Street*, November 2001.
2. Eric Lerner, *Matters of Vital Interest*, 131.
3. Scott, *Leonard, Marianne and Me*, 80.
4. Dimery, ed., *Leonard Cohen In His Own Words*, 89.
5. Posner, *The Early Years*, 461.
6. Ash, *Nomad Girl*, 161.
7. Avril Giacobbi, *The Judas Trail*, 52.
8. Dimery, ed., *Leonard Cohen In His Own Words*, 33.
9. Francis Mus, *The Demons of Leonard Cohen*, 79.
10. Tim Footman, *Hallelujah*, 83-4.

11. Steven Scobie, ed., *Intricate Preparations*, 114.
12. Evans, *An Illustrated Record*, 49.
13. Kubernick, *Everybody Knows*, 91.
14. Maurice Ratcliuffe, *Leonard Cohen: The Music and the Mystique*, 24.
15. Dimery, ed., *Leonard Cohen In His Own Words*, 67.
16. Michael Posner, *From This Broken Hill*, 5.
17. Fournier and Norris, *Take This Waltz*, 11.
18. *New Musical Express*, March 25, 1972.
19. *Mind of a Poet*.
20. Ash, *Nomad Girl*, 171.
21. *Elm Street*, November 2001.
22. Evans, *An Illustrated, Record*, 44.
23. Posner, *The Early Years*, 410.
24. Barrera, *Came So Far For Love*, 22.
25. *Macleans*, June 1972.
26. *Melody Maker*, April 1972.
27. Posner, *From This Broken Hill*, 196.
28. *Ibid.*, 212.
29. Harry Freedman, *Leonard Cohen: The Mystical Roots of Genius*, 25.
30. Matti Friedman, *Leonard Cohen in the Sinai*, 168.
31. Reynolds, *A Remarkable Life*, 209.
32. Footman, *Hallelujah*, 97.
33. Scott, *Leonard, Marianne and Me*, 37.
34. Colin Irwin, *Still the Man*, 119.
35. *Mind of a Poet*.
36. Harry Rasky, *The Song of Leonard Cohen*, 102.
37. *Ibid.*, 117.

38. Dimery, ed., *Leonard Cohen In His Own Words*, 43.
39. Posner, *The Early Years*, 292.
40. Cox and Sheddon, *Inside His Archive*, 120.

Spector of Doom

1. *Mojo*, January 2012.
2. Mick Brown, *Tearing Down the Wall of Sound: The Rise and Fall of Phil Spector*, 319.
3. *Ibid.*, 403.
4. *Ibid.*, 316.
5. Reynolds, *A Remarkable Life*, 139.
6. *Throat Culture*, 63.
7. *Uncut*, Ultimate Guide Series, 2017.
8. Reynolds, *A Remarkable Life*, 152.
9. *Ibid.*, 147.
10. *Mojo*, January 2012.
11. Dimery, ed., *Leonard Cohen In His Own Words*, 86.
12. Scobie, ed., *Intricate Preparations*, 133.
13. Christophe Lebold, *Leonard Cohen: The Man Who Saw the Angels Fall*, 235.
14. *Rolling Stone*, February 9, 1978.
15. *Hallelujah: A Journey, A Song*.
16. Brown, *Tearing Down the Wall of Sound*, 319-20.
17. Reynolds, *A Remarkable Life*, 159.
18. Kubernick, *Everybody Knows*, 123.

Crawling From the Wreckage

1. Howard Sounes, *Down the Highway: The Life of Bob Dylan*, 336.

2. Scott M. Marshall, *Bob Dylan: The Spiritual Life*, 78.
3. *Mojo*, January, 2012.
4. David Kenny, *The Little Buke of Dublin*, 60.
5. Posner, *From This Broken Hill*, 307.
6. *Mind of a Poet*.
7. *Newsday*, November 22, 1992.
8. *Sunday Independent*, August 11, 2019.
9. Posner, *That's How the Light Gets In*, 125.
10. *Mojo*, January 2012.
11. *Metro Times*, August 18, 1993.

Back in the Game
1. Nadel, *Various Positions*, 234.
2. *Ibid.*, 154.
3. *Hallelujah: A Journey, A Song*.
4. *Mind of a Poet*.
5. Nadel, *Various Positions*, 244.
6. Posner, *From This Broken Hill*, 399.

Dublin Visit
1. *In Dublin*, June 9, 1988.
2. *Women's Journal*, January 1980.
3. *In Dublin*, June 9, 1988.
4. *Ibid.*
5. *Ibid.*
6. *Ibid.*
7. Hodes, *The Water and the Wine*, 98.
8. *In Dublin*, June 9, 1988.

9. *Ibid.*
10. *Ibid.*
11. Irwin, *Still the Man*, 102.
12. *Blitz*, February, 1988.

Burn-Out

1. Simmons, *I'm Your Man*, 359.
2. *Ibid.*, 362.
3. Cox and Sheddon, *Inside His Archive*, 90.
4. Burger, *Leonard Cohen on Leonard Cohen*, 117.
5. Posner, *That's How the Light Gets In*, 385.
6. Ratcliffe, *The Music and the Mystique*, 51.
7. MacKenna, *Absent Friend*, 91.
8. *Interview*, June 1993.
9. *W5 CTV*, October 28, 1997.
10. Boucher and Boucher, *Deaths and Entrances*, 32.
11. Posner, *That's How the Light Gets In*, 154.
12. Dimery, ed., *Leonard Cohen In His Own Words*, 74.
13. Fournier and Norris, *Take This Waltz*, 113.
14. Lerner, *Matters of Vital Interest*, 177.
15. *Synergie*, October 6, 1997.
16. MacKenna, *Absent Friend*, 71.
17. Burger, *Leonard Cohen on Leonard Cohen*, 415.
18. Footman, *Hallelujah*, 140.
19. *Classic Interviews*.
20. *Q* magazine, April 1988.
21. Rasky, *The Song of Leonard Cohen*, 136.
22. Cox and Sheddon, *Inside His Archive*, 95.
23. *Saturday Night*, September 15, 2001.

24. Burger, *Leonard Cohen on Leonard Cohen*, 465.
25. *Mind of a Poet*.
26. Ted Kessler, ed., *My Old Man*, 140-1.
27. Chris Wade, *The Music of Leonard Cohen*, 99.
28. Roger Green, *Hydra and the Bananas of Leonard Cohen*.
29. *Globe and Mail*, May 26, 2007.
30. Posner, *That's How the Light Gets In, 327*.

The Deal is Rotten

1. *Billboard*, November 28, 1998.
2. Posner, *That's How the Light Gets In*, 273.
3. *Mind of a Poet*.
4. Light, *The Holy or the Broken*, 140.
5. Simmons, *I'm Your Man*, 426.
6. *Macleans*, June 12, 2008.
7. Lebold, *The Man Who Saw the Angels Fall*, 367.
8. He eventually thought of one - "door hinge" - but not many people were impressed with it.
9. Reynolds, *A Remarkable Life*, 283.

First We Take Fredericton

1. Lerner, *Matters of Vital Interest*, 195.
2. *Mojo*, January 2012.
3. Posner, *That's How the Light Gets In*, 316.
4. Lerner, *Matters of Vital Interest*, 196.
5. Irwin, *Still the Man*, 124.
6. Kessler, ed., *My Old Man*, 139.
7. Fournier and Norris, *Take This Waltz*, 155.

8. *Classic Interviews.*
9. Reynolds, *A Remarkable Life*, 299.
10. *Hallelujah: A Journey, A Song.*
11. *Ibid.*
12. Ratcliffe, *The Music and the Mystique*, 82.
13. *Hot Press*, Christmas 2016.
14. MacKenna, *Absent Friend*, 107-8.
15. Lerner, *Matters of Vital Interest*, 233.

Closing Time

1. *New Yorker*, October 17, 2016.
2. Lerner, *Matters of Vital Interest*, 244.
3. *Irish Times*, November 16, 2019.
4. *Mojo*, January 2012.
5. Posner, *That's How the Light Gets In*, 421.
6. *People*, November 11, 2016.
7. Posner, *That's How the Light Gets In*, 195.

Bibliography

Ash, Niema. *Nomad Girl: My Adventures with Bob Dylan, Leonard Cohen, John Lee Hooker, the Dalai Lama and More.* Leicestershire, UK: Matador, 2020.

Barrera, Paul. *Came So Far For Love: The Words and Music of Leonard Cohen.* Hampshire, UK: Agenda, 1997.

Boucher, David, and Lucy Boucher. *Bob Dylan and Leonard Cohen: Deaths and Entrances.* New York: Bloomsbury Academic, 2021.

Brown, Mick. *Tearing Down the Wall of Sound: The Rise and Fall of Phil Spector.* London: Bloomsbury, 2008.

Burger, Jeff, ed. *Leonard Cohen on Leonard Cohen.* London: Omnibus, 2014.

Cohen, Leonard. *Let Us Compare Mythologies.* Toronto: McClelland & Stewart, 1956.

- *The Spice Box of Earth.* Toronto: McClelland & Stewart, 1961.
- *The Favourite Game.* London: Blue Door, 1963.
- *Flowers for Hitler.* Toronto: McClelland and Stewart, 1964.
- *Beautiful Losers.* London: Panther, 1966.
- *Parasites of Heaven.* Toronto: McClelland & Stewart, 1966.
- *Selected Poems: 1956-1968.* Toronto: McClelland & Stewart, 1968.
- *The Energy of Slaves.* Toronto: McClelland & Stewart, 1972.
- *Death of a Lady's Man.* London: Andre Deutsch, 1978.

- *Book of Mercy*. Toronto: McClelland & Stewart, 1984.
- *Stranger Music: Selected Poems and Songs*. London: Jonathan Cape, 1993.
- *Book of Longing*. Toronto: McClelland & Stewart, 2006.
- *The Flame*. Edinburgh: Canongate, 2018.

Collins, Judy. *Sweet Judy Blue Eyes: My Life in Music*. New York: Three Rivers Press, 2011.

Cox, Julian, and Jim Sheddon. *Leonard Cohen, Everybody Knows: Inside His Archive*. New York: Art Gallery of Ontario.

Devlin, Jim. *In Every Style of Passion: The Works of Leonard Cohen*. London: Omnibus, 1996.

Dimery, Robert, ed. *Leonard Cohen In His Own Words*. London: Omnibus, 1998.

Dorman, L.S., and C.L. Rawlins. *Leonard Cohen: Prophet of the Heart*. London: Omnibus, 1990.

Evans, Mike. *Leonard Cohen: An Illustrated Record*. London: Plexus, 2018.

Footman, Tim. *Hallelujah*. Surrey, UK: Chrome Dreams, 2009.

Fournier, Michael and Ken Norris, eds., *Take This Waltz: A Celebration of Leonard Cohen*. Quebec: The Muses Company, 1994.

Freedman, Harry. *Leonard Cohen: The Mystical Roots of Genius*. London: Bloomsbury, 2024.

Friedman, Matti. *Leonard Cohen in the Sinai*. New York: Spiegel & Grau, 2022.

Giacobbi, Avril. *The Judas Trail*. Amazon, 2018.

Girard, Philippe. *Leonard Cohen On a Wire*. Quebec: Drawn and Quarterly, 2021.

Gnarowski, Michael, ed., *Leonard Cohen: The Artist and his Critics.* Toronto: McGraw-Hill, 1976.

Godden, Victoria, ed. *I'm Your Man: The Little Guide to Leonard Cohen.* London: Welbeck, 2022.

Green, Roger. *Hydra and the Bananas of Leonard Cohen.* New York: Perseus, 2003.

Hesthamar, Kari. *So Long Marianne: A Love Story.* Toronto: ECW Press, 2017.

Hodes, Tamar. *The Water and the Wine.* UK: Hookline Books, 2023.

Holt, Jason, ed. *Leonard Cohen and Philosophy.* Chicago, IL: Open Court Publishing, 2014.

Irwin, Colin. *Leonard Cohen: Still The Man.* London: Flame Tree Publishing, 2015.

Kessler, Ted. *My Old Man: Tales of Our Fathers.* Edinburgh: Canongate, 2017.

Kubernick, Harvey. *Leonard Cohen: Everybody Knows.* London: Omnibus, 2014.

Lebold, Christophe. *Leonard Cohen: The Man Who Saw the Angels Fall.* Toronto: ECW Press, 2018.

Leibovitz, Liel. *A Broken Hallelujah: Leonard Cohen's Secret Chord.* Dingwall, Scotland: Sandstone Press, 2014.

Lerner, Eric. *Matters of Vital Interest: A Forty-Year Friendship with Leonard Cohen.* New York: Da Capo, 2018.

Lewis, Jeffrey. *Leonard Cohen: A Novel.* London: Haus Publishing, 2024.

Light, Alan. *The Holy or the Broken: Leonard Cohen, Jeff Buckley and the Unlikely Ascent of "Hallelujah."* New York: Atria, 2012.

Machat, Steven. *Gods, Gangsters and Honour.* Glasgow: McNae, Marlin & Mackenzie, 2022.

MacKenna, John. *Absent Friend: A Meditation on a Friendship with Leonard Cohen.* Harvest Press, 2023.

Mus, Francis. *The Demons of Leonard Cohen.* Ottawa: University of Ottawa Press, 2020.

Nadel, Ira B. *Various positions: A Life of Leonard Cohen.* London: Bloomsbury, 1997.

Nonnekes, Paul. *Three Moments of Love in Leonard Cohen and Bruce Cockburn.* Montreal, Canada: Black Rose Books, 2001.

O'Brien, Karen. *Joni Mitchell: Shadows and Light.* London: Virgin, 2002.

Posner, Michael. *Untold Stories: The Early Years.* New York: Simon & Schuster, 2020.

- *From This Broken Hill.* New York: Simon & Schuster, 2021.
- *That's How the Light Gets In.* New York: Simon & Schuster, 2022.

Rasky, Harry. *The Song of Leonard Cohen.* London: Souvenir Press, 2010.

Ratcliffe, Maurice. *Leonard Cohen: The Music and the Mystique.* London: Omnibus, 2012.

Reynolds, Anthony. *Leonard Cohen: A Remarkable Life.* London: Omnibus, 2010.

Robinson, Sharon. *On Tour with Leonard Cohen.* New York: Powerhouse Books, 2014.

Samson, Polly. *A Theatre for Dreamers.* London: Bloomsbury, 2021.

Scobie, Stephen, ed., *Intricate Preparations: Writing Leonard Cohen.* Toronto: ECW, 2000.

Scott, Judy. *Leonard, Marianne and Me.* Lanham, MD: Rowman & Littlefield, 2021.

Simmons, Sylvie. *I'm Your Man: The Life of Leonard Cohen.* London: Vintage.

Sounes, Howard. *Down the Highway: The Life of Bob Dylan.* London: Black Swan, 2002.

Walker, George A. *A Woodcut Biography.* Ontario: Firefly Books, 2020.

Warhol, Andy and Pat Hackett. *POPism: The Warhol Sixties.* London: Penguin, 1980.

DVDs

Ladies and Gentlemen...Mr Leonard Cohen (National Film Board of Canada, 1965)

I Am a Hotel (CBC 1984)

I'm Your Man (Metropolitan Video, 2005)

Leonard Cohen's Lonesome Heroes (Pride Productions, 2010).

Bird on a Wire (Machat company, 2013)

The Mind of a Poet: Interviews and Contributions (LV Production, 2015)

Marianne and Leonard: Words of Love (Dogwoof, 2019)

Hallelujah: Leonard Cohen: A Journey, a Song (Sony, 2021) CD

The Classic Interviews (Chrome Dreams)